GOSPEL SHAPED

MERCY

Handbook

GOSPEL SHAPED

MERCY

Stephen Um

Gospel Shaped Mercy Handbook
© The Gospel Coalition / The Good Book Company 2017

Published by:
The Good Book Company
Tel (US): 866 244 2165
Tel (UK): 0333 123 0880
Email (US): info@thegoodbook.com
Email (UK): info@thegoodbook.co.uk

Websites:
North America: www.thegoodbook.com
UK: www.thegoodbook.co.uk
Australia: www.thegoodbook.com.au
New Zealand: www.thegoodbook.co.nz

ISBN: 9781909919532 Printed in India

PRODUCTION TEAM:

AUTHOR:
Stephen Um

**SERIES EDITOR FOR
THE GOSPEL COALITION:**
Collin Hansen

**SERIES EDITOR FOR
THE GOOD BOOK COMPANY:**
Tim Thornborough

**MAIN TEACHING SESSION
DISCUSSIONS:** Alison Mitchell

DAILY DEVOTIONALS:
Tim Thornborough

BIBLE STUDIES:
Tim Thornborough

EDITORIAL ASSISTANTS:
Jeff Robinson (TGC), Rachel Jones (TGBC)

VIDEO EDITOR:
Phil Grout

PROJECT ADMINISTRATOR:
Jackie Moralee

EXECUTIVE PRODUCER:
Brad Byrd

DESIGN:
André Parker

CONTENTS

SERIES PREFACE   7

INTRODUCTION   9

HOW TO USE GOSPEL SHAPED MERCY   11

SESSIONS

SESSION 1: SHALOM:
THE WORLD MADE BEAUTIFUL   13

SESSION 2: JUSTICE:
WRONGS MADE RIGHT   33

SESSION 3: LOVE:
THE HEART OF COMPASSION   53

SESSION 4: MERCY:
HEARTS MADE SOFT   73

SESSION 5: GENEROSITY:
STEWARDING GOD'S MONEY   93

SESSION 6: RECONCILIATION:
RELATIONSHIPS HEALED   113

SESSION 7: DIVERSITY:
COMMUNITY ENRICHED   133

 **PREFACE**

GROWING A GOSPEL SHAPED CHURCH

The Gospel Coalition is a group of pastors and churches in the Reformed heritage who delight in the truth and power of the gospel, and who want the gospel of Christ crucified and resurrected to lie at the center of all we cherish, preach and teach.

We want churches called into existence by the gospel to be shaped by the gospel in their everyday life.

Through our fellowship, conferences, and online and printed media, we have sought to encourage pastors and church leaders to calibrate their lives around what is of first importance—the gospel of Christ. In these resources, we want to provide those same pastors with the tools to excite and equip church members with this mindset.

In our foundation documents, we identified five areas that should mark the lives of believers in a local fellowship:

1. Empowered corporate worship
2. Evangelistic effectiveness
3. Counter-cultural community
4. The integration of faith and work
5. The doing of justice and mercy

We believe that a church utterly committed to winsome and theologically substantial expository preaching, and that lives out the gospel in these areas, will display its commitment to dynamic evangelism, apologetics, and church planting. These gospel-shaped churches will emphasize repentance, personal renewal, holiness, and the wonderful life of the church as the body of Christ. At the same time, there will be engagement with the social structures of ordinary people; and cultural engagement with art, business, scholarship and government. The church will be characterized by firm devotion to the truth on the one hand, and by transparent compassion on the other.

The Gospel Coalition believes in the priority of the local church, and that the local church is the best place to discuss these five ministry drivers and decide how to integrate them into life and mission. So, while being clear on the biblical principles, these resources give space to consider what a genuine expression of a gospel-shaped church looks like for you in the place where God has put you, and with the people he has gathered into fellowship with you.

Through formal teaching sessions, daily Bible devotionals, group Bible studies and the regular preaching ministry, it is our hope and prayer that congregations will grow into maturity, and so honor and glorify our great God and Savior.

Don Carson
President

Tim Keller
Vice President

INTRODUCTION

We live in a broken, fractured world that is hungry for the love and grace of Christ.

Many churches are committed to worship, evangelism and Bible ministry—but when it comes to getting involved in works of mercy and compassion, we're a little more hesitant. Will it somehow take us away from the Bible's call to make disciples?

But the gospel calls us to works of mercy and compassion. It's an integral part of our witness to the wider world.

The Christian gospel is wonderful good news for the poor, marginalized and oppressed: God has a plan to restore our troubled world into one of flourishing, beauty, justice and fullness. And the thrilling news for us is that Christ wants his church to be an active part of that plan too.

The Gospel Coalition has included this statement in their Theological Vision for Ministry, entitled "The doing of Justice and Mercy." It begins:

> God created both soul and body, and the resurrection of Jesus shows that he is going to redeem both the spiritual and the material. Therefore God is concerned not only for the salvation of souls but also for the relief of poverty, hunger, and injustice…

And it concludes that both as individual Christians and as whole churches, we have a divine calling to practically demonstrate God's love for the world:

> We must work for the eternal and common good and show our neighbors we love them sacrificially whether they believe as we do or not. Indifference to the poor and disadvantaged means there has not been a true grasp of our salvation by sheer grace…[1]

Historically, the Christian church has been in the forefront of showing concern for the poor and needy. From the earliest times, Christians cared for widows. They took in and cared for abandoned orphans. They founded hospitals and cared for the sick, they visited those in prison and they brought relief to the poor. And in more recent times, they have championed social reform to improve life in prisons

---

[1] You can read the full text of the statement on page 158

and end slavery, and have fought for laws that outlaw the exploitation of the poor and helpless.

But more recently, there has been a growing suspicion among evangelical churches about the place of justice and mercy in their everyday congregational life. They have seen that some churches, and even whole denominations have eagerly embraced the call to do mercy, but seem to have lost their passion for sharing the gospel of forgiveness of sins through Jesus. They have concluded that this area of Christian life and witness is something to be wary of.

True, there are dangers. But, as we will see in this series, God's call to show his love, justice and mercy to our needy world, is both clear and uncompromising.

You might be unsettled as you work through this material and see significant areas where you and your church are holding back from the clear commands of Scripture. Don't give up or try to avoid what the Lord needs to reveal within you and your church. Instead, prayerfully work through these sessions with the happy and humble confidence that God wants to use you in bringing the light of the gospel to our world.

Over the seven sessions of *Gospel Shaped Mercy* we'll explore God's breathtaking vision for a world put right. And we'll get practical too, as we discuss how your church community can better show the justice, love and mercy of Christ to those around you.

Stephen Um

HOW TO USE GOSPEL SHAPED MERCY

MAIN TEACHING SESSION This session combines watching short talks on a DVD or listening to "live" talks with times for discussion. These prompt you to think about what you have heard and how it might apply to your church and cultural context. Bear in mind that there is not necessarily a "right answer" to every question!

DEVOTIONALS Each session comes with six daily personal devotionals. These look at passages that are linked to the theme of the Main Teaching Session, and are for you to read and meditate on at home through the week after the session. You may like to do them in addition to or instead of your usual daily devotionals, or use them to begin such a practice.

JOURNAL As you reflect on what you have learned as a group and in your personal devotionals, use this page to record the main truths that have struck you, things you need to pray about, and issues you'd like to discuss further or questions you'd like to ask.

BIBLE STUDY As part of this curriculum, your church may be running weekly Bible Studies as well as the Main Teaching Sessions. These look more closely at a passage and help you focus on an aspect of the Main Teaching Session. If your church is not using this part of the curriculum, you could work through it on your own or with another church member.

SERMON NOTES Your church's preaching program may be following this curriculum; space has been provided for you to make notes on these sermons in your Handbook.

SESSION 1:

SHALOM: THE WORLD MADE BEAUTIFUL

AT THE BEGINNING OF THE BIBLE, WE GET A BREATHTAKING VISION OF THE WAY THE WORLD IS MEANT TO BE. IT'S A PLACE OF WHOLENESS, FLOURISHING AND FULLNESS – IN OTHER WORDS, SHALOM. BUT AS WE LOOK AT THE WORLD AROUND US TODAY, WE SEE BROKENNESS, HURT AND EXPLOITATION. WHY? AND WHAT IS GOD DOING ABOUT IT? IN THIS SESSION WE'LL SEE WHAT GOD HAS DONE, AND IS DOING, TO RESTORE SHALOM TO HIS CREATION.

SHALOM: THE WORLD MADE BEAUTIFUL

Discuss

What comes into your mind when you hear the word *shalom*?

_____

_____

_____

_____

▶ WATCH DVD 1.1 OR LISTEN TO TALK 1.1

_____

_____

_____

_____

_____

_____

Discuss

"Shalom *is both the absence of conflict and the presence of wholeness.*"
Which part of this definition do you find most appealing, and why?

_____

_____

_____

"Shalom *is shorthand for the way the world is meant to be."* Do you find this a helpful summary? Why / why not?

_____

_____

_____

_____

▶ **WATCH DVD 1.2 OR LISTEN TO TALK 1.2**

_____

_____

_____

_____

_____

_____

_____

_____

_____

_____

_____

_____

_____

_____

_____

_____

 **GENESIS 1:26-28**

> [26] Then God said, "Let us make man in our image, after our likeness. And let them have dominion over the fish of the sea and over the birds of the heavens and over the livestock and over all the earth and over every creeping thing that creeps on the earth." [27] So God created man in his own image, in the image of God he created him; male and female he created them. [28] And God blessed them. And God said to them, "Be fruitful and multiply and fill the earth and subdue it, and have dominion over the fish of the sea and over the birds of the heavens and over every living thing that moves on the earth."

Discuss

"Humans are the only creatures created in the image of God. That means we have an inherent dignity that is different from everything else. This is the grounding principle for everything we are going to consider about social justice, mercy and compassion."

Why do you think our role as image-bearers is so important for how we think about social justice, mercy and compassion?

_____

_____

_____

_____

As God's image-bearers, Adam and Eve were meant to be royal caretakers of the world (Genesis 1:28). How did they fail at this task? (See Genesis 2:15-17 and 3:6.)

_____

_____

_____

_____

_____

Jesus was the Royal Caretaker of the world. How did he succeed at this task? (See Genesis 3:15 and Colossians 1:19-20.)

_____

_____

_____

_____

"*Sin vandalizes shalom and destroys it.*" Can you think of some examples of this in your home, your neighborhood, and your country?

_____

_____

_____

_____

▶ **WATCH DVD 1.3 OR LISTEN TO TALK 1.3**

_____

_____

_____

_____

_____

_____

_____

_____

_____

_____

_____

_____

Discuss

"The Christian experience of shalom *is held in an 'already/not yet' tension."* Complete the table below to see some examples of this.

ALREADY	NOT YET
Jesus has already made peace by his blood	
Jesus has already defeated death by his own death and resurrection	
	Jesus is coming back to finally establish *shalom*
Christians are already adopted by God	
	In the new creation all things will be made new

While we wait for Jesus to return, we live in a fallen world. We don't fully experience *shalom*. What difference does it make to our daily lives that we can be confident that one day we will experience full, lasting *shalom*?

Pray

 **REVELATION 21:1-5**

> *¹ Then I saw a new heaven and a new earth, for the first heaven and the first earth had passed away, and the sea was no more. ² And I saw the holy city, new Jerusalem, coming down out of heaven from God, prepared as a bride adorned for her husband. ³ And I heard a loud voice from the throne saying, "Behold, the dwelling place of God is with man. He will dwell with them, and they will be his people, and God himself will be with them as their God. ⁴ He will wipe away every tear from their eyes, and death shall be no more, neither shall there be mourning, nor crying, nor pain anymore, for the former things have passed away." ⁵ And he who was seated on the throne said, "Behold, I am making all things new."*

LOOK FORWARD to the coming of the new creation, when there will be no more death, mourning, crying or pain. Thank God that you have such perfect *shalom* to look forward to.

LOOK BACK to the death and resurrection of Jesus, which makes this perfect *shalom* possible. Thank God for sending his own Son, Jesus, to do this for us.

LOOK AROUND at your group, your church and your neighborhood. Ask God to help your church family to live in a way that honors him and brings *shalom* as far as you are able to.

DAILY BIBLE DEVOTIONALS

The world was created good, but the fall has stripped *shalom* from every area of life: spiritually, relationally, in creation, in our institutions, and in ourselves personally.

Day 1

GENESIS 3:8-24

"What is this that you have done?"

After the man and woman ate the fruit from the forbidden tree:

Q: *What details point to the separation that now exists between man and God?*

Q: *What details point to God's continuing love for them and future plans?*

The man and woman hid from God, but were then cursed and expelled from Eden as the inevitable consequence of grasping at being like God. But woven throughout are indications of his love: he made clothes for them; he promised the crushing of the serpent; and even the expulsion from Eden can be seen as protecting them from a more damaging act of rebellion.

Our problem is not so much that we *break* rules; it is that we feel free to *make* rules—as though we know better than God. Every one of us is born into Adam's sinful mindset, and experiences separation from God as a result.

PRAY: *Almighty God, thank you that you love and care for me, even though I have rebelled against you. Help me to face up to my sin and to rejoice in your love for sinners like me. Amen.*

Day 2

EPHESIANS 2:1-3

"You were dead…"

Not just separated from God in the way we might be apart from a friend for a while. The consequences of sin are much, much greater.

Q: *What "trinity of evil" is at work in our lives in these verses?*

Q: *What is the ultimate consequence (v 3)?*

The world, the flesh and the devil all work together to confirm our sinful status. The world squeezes us into its mold, and the devil whispers temptations in our ears. We complain, "It's not my fault!" but we are wrong. The world and the devil are just encouraging us to do *what we want.* Our bodily desires and corrupt minds (v 3) are happy to listen to temptation, and to go along with the way the world works. The tragic consequence for all mankind is that we are subject to the wrath of God.

This grim picture should leave us lost and depressed, but before you pray, take a look at verses 4 and 5 for some hope…

PRAY: *Lord, I am lost without you. I listen to the devil's lies; I give in to the pressure of the world; I have a corrupt mind and heart. But thank you that you have not left me there.*

Day 3

GENESIS 3:17-18; ROMANS 8:18-23

"Cursed is the ground because of you…"

It's easy to detect how sin has vandalized the *shalom* of creation. Anyone with a garden knows about weeds. But it runs so much deeper…

Q: *Read Romans 8:18-23. How does creation "feel"? Why?*

Q: *What is the ultimate destiny of creation? How does it share this with Christians?*

There is nothing more glorious and awe-inspiring than an amazing sunset, a dramatic cliff-top view or a star-filled sky. And yet this is creation *frustrated*! It does not work as it should (earthquakes, tsunamis, storms); it is not as beautiful as it should be. And when it is pillaged by humankind, it can be downright ugly.

But that is not its end. This passage promises a more glorious future. Just as creation has been caught up in the fall with men and women, so it will be caught up in redemption and fulfillment with those who belong to Jesus. Imagine the Grand Canyon—but better! But for now, the experience is one of frustration and eager waiting. For now we must care for creation—the land, the air, the animal world—and steward it as a resource; but we know that though it shares in our ruin, it will be part of our more glorious future.

PRAY: *Thank God for the joy and beauty of creation, and ask for his help to be a responsible steward of our frustrated world.*

Day 4

DANIEL 3:1-18; ROMANS 13:1

"Nebuchadnezzar made an image of gold…"

It is in the nature of governments to outstrip their authority, because governments are made up of sinful, fallen people, whose instinct is, like Nebuchadnezzar, to play God. And yet the Bible is consistent in urging us to be subject to authorities—even when they are bad, wrong and oppressive.

Q: *Read Romans 13:1. Why are we to be subject to authorities?*

Q: *Where have you seen the fall evidenced at all levels of government?*

It's not just the high-profile scandals of corrupt leaders, or the power-hungry dictators that show the institutional effects of sin. We see it in the minor official who denies a request just because they can, or the poor administration of a local school, or the lax performance of refuse collectors. But how do Christians live in a world like this—filled with minor frustrations?

We live in the "in-between times"—after Christ has won redemption on the cross, but before that redemption is fully revealed when he returns. Christians are called to be obedient to government and to pray for our leaders. We both understand the fallenness of *all* human institutions and also have a deep trust in the sovereignty of God over all things.

PRAY: *Pray you would honor your government, and work to encourage and improve it.*

Day 5

GENESIS 4; PHILIPPIANS 2:1-11

"Cain rose up against his brother Abel and killed him."

Murder is perhaps the ultimate expression of the breakdown of a relationship, and it's right there in the chapter following the description of the fall. Subsequently, we repeatedly read about disastrous marriages, ruined relationships and failed families. A family is where the fruitful flourishing of *shalom* should be most evident; but we could list countless examples of failure from Cain and Abel, Noah and Abraham through to David and Solomon, and their successors. We are the same today.

Q: *Why are the commands of Philippians 2:3-4 so difficult for us to keep?*

Q: *Where do Christians look for our example for good relationships?*

While we live in the "in-between times," there will be a constant need for forgiveness, humility and self-sacrifice, if we are to work against our sinful instinct to fall out with people and divide. While Adam and all who follow him grasp for God-like power to make the rules and get the glory, Jesus was willing to let go of it all, in order to love us, serve us, and ultimately rescue us. We must expect sin-riddled relationships to be difficult. But in Christ we have both his example and the Spirit's power to live differently.

PRAY: *Thank you, Lord, for my friends and family. Help me to follow Jesus as I seek to live in peace and love with them. Amen.*

Day 6

PSALM 34:15-22

In this world broken things are just thrown away; damaged goods are rejected. Our world is full of people with broken hearts, broken spirits and broken relationships.

Q: *What bitter truths does this psalm acknowledge are a real part of our lives?*

Q: *What encouragements are there for us as we wrestle with this reality?*

Brokenness shows itself in a thousand small ways every day. How we think; how we talk; the decisions we make; the things we ignore; the things we get obsessed with. Brokenness is easy to spot at the extremes, with mental breakdowns, an inability to form or keep relationships, or in drug or alcohol abuse. But it is a subtle ever-present reality in all of us, which we do well to acknowledge before the Lord and each other.

The wonderful promise is that the Lord is close to us when we are at our most downcast and most defeated. When we reach our lowest point, he is there waiting for us, assuring us of his love and understanding, and the security of our status with him.

Q: *How can you show the Lord's mercy and grace to people you know who are brokenhearted or spirit-crushed (v 18)?*

PRAY: *Thank you, Father, that you are close to me in Christ—especially when I am at my weakest. Please give me opportunities today to share your loving concern and support with those I meet and spend time with. Amen.*

 **JOURNAL**

What I've learned or been particularly struck by this week…

What I want to change in my perspectives or actions as a result of this week…

Things I would like to think about more or discuss with others at my church…

BIBLE STUDY

Discuss

If you asked people in the street to describe the world they would love to live in, what kind of answers would they give? What does this show about people in general?

👉 READ REVELATION 21:1-8; 22:1-5

¹ Then I saw a new heaven and a new earth, for the first heaven and the first earth had passed away, and the sea was no more…

1. What surprises you about this new world (21:1-2)?

2. What will this new world be like? How is it like the picture of Eden in Genesis 2?

Why are these qualities of eternal life so attractive to us?

3. Who is at the center of this new world?

4. In the death of Jesus, we have been shown justice, mercy, compassion and inclusion. Christians have always worked to model these qualities in their personal lives, in the lives of their churches, and in the wider world. Where have Christians gone wrong when thinking about working for these qualities in these three areas? How does Revelation help us with this issue?

5. How will the sure promise of the new creation help us when:

   ● we are tempted to give up our faith because of opposition?

   ● we want to give up working for justice, inclusion and mercy in a world that is unfair?

   ● we are overwhelmed by the needs we see in our world?

6. How can this understanding of where we have come from and where we are going help us share the gospel with others?

_____

_____

_____

_____

_____

Apply

FOR YOURSELF: Which aspect of our fallenness do you feel most keenly? Which aspect of the new creation are you most looking forward to? Do you think you are involved too much or too little in working in your family, neighborhood or world to pursue *shalom*?

_____

_____

_____

_____

_____

FOR YOUR CHURCH: Do you think this area of our gospel response is too small or too great as a congregation? What are you hoping to get out of this series as you study, think, discuss and pray together?

_____

_____

_____

_____

Pray

FOR YOUR GROUP: Ask God to fill you with a sense of assurance and joy about his promise that all things will be made new in the new creation.

FOR YOUR CHURCH: Pray that, both as individuals and as a church, you would find ways to express the justice, mercy, inclusion and compassion you have experienced in the gospel, both to each other, and to the wider world.

SERMON NOTES

Bible passage: Date:

SESSION 2:

JUSTICE: WRONGS MADE RIGHT

LAST SESSION WE LOOKED AT GOD'S PROMISE OF A FUTURE WORLD MADE WHOLE AND BEAUTIFUL. BUT WHAT DOES GOD WANT HIS PEOPLE TO DO AS WE WAIT, LIVING IN THE TENSION BETWEEN THE "NOW" AND THE "NOT YET"? IN THIS SESSION, WE'LL HEAR GOD'S CALL TO HIS PEOPLE TO "DO JUSTICE" – TO WORK TO MAKE RIGHT THE WRONGS OF OUR WORLD.

JUSTICE: WRONGS MADE RIGHT

Discuss

What comes into your mind when you hear the word "justice"?

_____

_____

_____

_____

Think about the people in your neighborhood. Do you think they would associate your church or group with caring about justice? Why / why not?

_____

_____

_____

_____

▶ **WATCH DVD 2.1 OR LISTEN TO TALK 2.1**

_____

_____

_____

_____

_____

_____

_____

_____

AMOS 5:21-23

21 I hate, I despise your feasts,
   and I take no delight in your solemn assemblies.
22 Even though you offer me your burnt offerings and grain offerings,
   I will not accept them;
and the peace offerings of your fattened animals,
   I will not look upon them.
23 Take away from me the noise of your songs;
   to the melody of your harps I will not listen.

Discuss

These words were written nearly 2,800 years ago. Who do you think they apply to today?

_____

_____

_____

_____

▶ WATCH DVD 2.2 OR LISTEN TO TALK 2.2

_____

_____

_____

_____

_____

_____

_____

_____

_____

Discuss

The way the Israelites were acting in Amos 5:21-23 can be described as "empty religiosity." In what way was their religious activity "empty," and how did God respond to it?

_____

_____

_____

_____

_____

AMOS 5:24

²⁴ But let justice roll down like waters,
and righteousness like an ever-flowing stream.

What do we learn about justice from this verse?

_____

_____

_____

_____

_____

"God desires neither faithless justice nor justice-less faith." While this sentence describes two extremes, the reality is often more subtle. In what ways do you see these two alternatives play out in your own experience?

_____

_____

_____

_____

▶ **WATCH DVD 2.3 OR LISTEN TO TALK 2.3**

_____

_____

_____

_____

_____

_____

_____

_____

_____

_____

_____

_____

_____

☞ **PSALM 146:5-9**

⁵ Blessed is he whose help is the God of Jacob,
    whose hope is in the LORD his God,
⁶ who made heaven and earth,
    the sea, and all that is in them,
who keeps faith forever;
⁷   who executes justice for the oppressed,
    who gives food to the hungry.
The LORD sets the prisoners free;
⁸   the LORD opens the eyes of the blind.
The LORD lifts up those who are bowed down;
    the LORD loves the righteous.
⁹ The LORD watches over the sojourners;
    he upholds the widow and the fatherless,
    but the way of the wicked he brings to ruin.

Discuss

Discuss the questions raised in the talk (printed below). If you don't have time to discuss them all, choose two or three categories where you think you or your church may be weak.

Verse 7, the oppressed:

● Who in your church or neighborhood is experiencing vocational, financial, or relational hardship? How can you or your church address their needs?

_____

_____

_____

Verse 7, prisoners:

● Are there those in your community who are literally imprisoned? Not just those in jail, but perhaps housebound or subject to domestic slavery? How might you and your church witness to the freedom of the gospel? How might you act as an advocate for the well-being of those that society has chosen to forget?

_____

_____

_____

Verse 8, the blind (the sick):

● Who in your community or church is in need of physical assistance? How can you help to alleviate their suffering, whether permanent or temporary, and help them back toward health in its widest sense?

_____

_____

_____

Verse 9, the sojourners (the outsiders):

- Are there those in your community who are not at "home" for one reason or another? They may be literally homeless, or have immigrated from another country, or are simply a community outsider. The question is: how can we make space for them in the warm, rather than leave them out in the cold?

Verse 9, the widows and fatherless:

- Who in your community experiences personal difficulty because of their relational situation? Are there single, divorced, or widowed people in need of assistance or friendship? Are there children who need physical, emotional and relational support and encouragement?

Beyond your neighborhood:

- The five sets of questions above all apply to your local community, but sometimes we will want to think more widely than that. What kind of issues do you think it is legitimate for Christians to campaign and fight for on the national stage, or internationally? How can you encourage those things to happen in your church, in a way that keeps a gospel perspective on the whole ministry?

_____

_____

_____

_____

_____

_____

_____

Pray

"God's justice is beautifully on display in the gospel. We see how seriously he takes sin, and how much he desires to embrace sinners. In Jesus, he does both."

Thank God for displaying his justice in the gospel.

Look again at your answers on pages 39 and 40. Ask God to help you put these into action.

DAILY BIBLE DEVOTIONALS

Throughout the pages of the Bible we discover a God who loves justice. These daily readings will help train us to love justice like our Father.

Day 1

ACTS 17:29-31

Paul is preaching to pagans who have never heard of Jesus. His attractive and reasonable sermon closes with a sharp call to them to change their minds about who God is.

Q: *What reasons does he give for their need to change (v 31)?*

Q: *What proof does he offer for this?*

The world today sees everything as a result of chance. It says, "We are here by a cosmic accident; our culture is built on invented rules—there is no such thing as absolute right and wrong." The Bible says something different. There is an absolute right and wrong that is determined not by the will of the people but by the will of God. And, like it or not, there is a judgment coming when *everything* will be put right.

People everywhere are instinctively hungry for justice; we know, deep down, that there is a judgment coming, but we suppress that knowledge (see Romans 1:18-20). That's why a gospel message that is faithful to this truth will always be met with hostility from many who are hiding from their own guilt, but will be embraced by a few (see Acts 17 v 31).

PRAY: *Ask the Lord to help you share the good news with others today.*

Day 2

MICAH 6:6-8

Important question: What truly pleases God?

Q: *What might the modern equivalents of verses 6 and 7 be?*

Q: *What is the real answer (v 8)? How do the different verbs before "justice," "kindness" and "humbly" show how this response to God is all-encompassing?*

Christian spirituality can easily become just about my feelings and internal state; or about just the things I do; or about just having a particular attitude or demeanor. These are all perversions of true religion, which must involve head, heart and hands together. Justice is something that should not just be felt, but *done*. We must feel kindness from our guts. Humility before God and others must be part of every interaction with others in the world.

And the perfect model for all of this is the Lord Jesus, who spoke and acted with great justice; who loved to show love and kindness to others; and who humbled himself even to death on a cross. This is what God requires of us; and it's a tall order. It takes a whole lifetime to work at in fact. A lifetime that starts right now.

PRAY: *Which of these areas do you feel most deficient in at the moment? Ask God to help you grow in it today.*

Day 3

LEVITICUS 19:1-2; 9-15

Q: *What is the fundamental reason why God's people should do all the things that follow in this chapter (v 1)?*

Q: *What two issues are highlighted in verse 15?*

Have we "privatized" holiness too much—so that it is just a matter of my own personal life, and less about how I treat others and the world? The commandments given here give shape to the variety of ways we need to be holy by actively seeking justice for others.

Being fair to my family and friends and at work are important. And how the justice system of our nation works also ought to be of concern. It should not matter whether we are poor or rich; we should get equal treatment under the law. When someone is acquitted because they were able to pay for slick lawyers, we should be ashamed of our system. When the poor are treated badly, we should likewise grieve, and work to change things in whatever way we can. Why? Because God is a God of justice, and Christians will strive to be like him. Ultimately, we can be reassured that no one will get away with anything, but that should not prevent us from working for justice now.

PRAY: *Lord, I pray for those who work for justice in our country: police, lawyers, judges, and the government. Help them to work for righteous justice that is fair for all.*

Day 4

PROVERBS 17:5

Q: *What's the connection between mocking the poor and insulting God?*

Q: *What kind of calamity or disaster do you think the proverb-writer had in mind? Why is gloating over it reprehensible?*

We judge people all the time. We log their clothing, speech, looks and demeanor, and then rapidly categorize about race and class, threat and attraction. And that's where it all goes wrong—unless we keep at the center of our minds the fundamental fact that we are all created equal and in the image of God; and we are therefore of equal value.

Likewise, if we believe that our Father orders the world for the glory of Christ and the advancement of the gospel, we can never see disasters of any kind as something to gloat over. We might say, or secretly think, "They deserved it"; or "That's what happens when you pursue that way of life." The truth is, we all deserve judgment, and it is only by grace that believers are spared the wrath of God to come. Rather, we should see disaster as an opportunity to repent, pray, and seek to show the love of Christ to our fellow sufferers in our sin-riddled world (see Luke 13:1-6).

Q: *How should this truth shape your prayers when you hear news of a tragedy or natural disaster?*

PRAY: *Lord, help me to look on others as made by you and therefore precious and equal. Amen.*

Day 5

ISAIAH 9:6-7

Isaiah foretells the birth of a child who will rule forever: Jesus. Verse 6 lists his titles and status, and verse 7 describes the quality of his reign.

Q: *What qualities are at the heart of the way Jesus rules?*

Q: *Why are these such attractive qualities for those who live in our world?*

Most of us live in countries where the civilized basics are taken for granted. But you don't have to look very hard to find places where life is oppressive and bitter because justice is arbitrary and irrational, or can be bought and sold.

Jesus our King zealously exercises all his authority and wisdom to create a kingdom that is just and righteous. And wherever the gospel is planted, Jesus' justice and righteousness will grow as his people seek to follow him. When we work for what is right and true and fair, we are expressing the rule of the Lord Jesus in just a small way. We show that his kingdom is the best place to live.

We can work for justice in many ways: by resolving children's arguments fairly; arguing for fairer policies at work; defending people unjustly accused; and by supporting agencies that work for justice worldwide. Whenever we do these things, we are working for and with the Lord Jesus, and looking toward the coming of his kingdom in all its fullness.

PRAY: *Thank you, Lord Jesus, that you rule the world. Help me extend your just and righteous rule in my life today. Amen.*

Day 6

PROVERBS 31:8-9

Q: *Who were these words originally addressed to (see v 1)?*

Q: *What are they calling us to do?*

It was very specifically the job of the king to speak up for the rights of the destitute, to defend the poor and needy. The people who do not have a voice need someone to speak up on their behalf.

It is right to apply this encouragement to ourselves, and not just to politicians. Yes, like Lemuel's mother (v 1), we should be urging our rulers not to forget the poor and destitute. Our justice systems need to protect as well as prosecute. But we all have a duty of care toward those who cannot take care of themselves. And when we see something that is wrong or unjust, we need to know that *silence is a sin*. When we turn a deaf ear to an injustice, we are turning a deaf ear to God's word, which is detestable to our just and loving God (see Proverbs 28:9). This determined outrage against injustice was what drove the great Christian reformers like Wilberforce, Lord Shaftesbury and Elizabeth Fry. They not only spoke up for the voiceless, but they did something about it.

Q: *Is this godly passion for justice something that you need to nurture in your heart and life? Start by speaking up.*

PRAY: *Lord, give me your heart of justice. Give me a voice that is willing to speak up for the poor and needy. Give me hands willing to work to see your will done. Amen.*

JOURNAL

What I've learned or been particularly struck by this week…

What I want to change in my perspectives or actions as a result of this week…

Things I would like to think about more or discuss with others at my church…

BIBLE STUDY

Discuss

From an early age, children will complain, "It's not fair!" Why do you think this sense of justice is so powerful in us? How does our sense of justice quickly go wrong?

READ AMOS 5:4-15

> [15] *Hate evil, and love good, and establish justice in the gate;*
> *it may be that the LORD, the God of hosts,*
> *will be gracious to the remnant of Joseph.*

1. What aspects of God's character are underlined in this passage?

_____

_____

_____

How do God's people stack up against this list?

_____

_____

_____

2. What is the point being made in verse 13? Why is that so terrible?

_____

_____

_____

_____

_____

3. What appeal is made to the people in v 14-15? Why is that so generous?

READ AMOS 5:21-24

21 I hate, I despise your feasts,
   and I take no delight in your solemn assemblies.

4. How does God view their religion? Why does he take their failings so seriously?

How does the vehemence of this language make you feel? What should it lead us to do?

5. What might a Christian believer, and a church, that is working to realize verse 24 look like?

_____

_____

_____

How does James 1:27 confirm that this is part of Christian discipleship?

_____

_____

_____

Apply

FOR YOURSELF: Discuss in what common ways you are tempted to act unjustly in your families, at work, or in the wider community. How can you start to let justice roll on like a river in your lives?

_____

_____

_____

_____

IN YOUR NATION: In what ways can you personally impact and fight injustice on a national and international level?

_____

_____

_____

FOR YOUR CHURCH: How can a church fellowship live out verse 24 in its congregational life? Be very practical!

_____

_____

_____

_____

Pray

FOR YOUR GROUP: Pray that you would have a deeper understanding of how deep and wide God's love of justice and righteousness is. Use your answers to question 2 to inform your prayers.

FOR YOURSELF: If you are facing injustice or oppression yourself, pray for those who are responsible, and cry to God for justice.

FOR YOUR CHURCH: Pray that as individuals, and as a church, you would have a growing commitment to justice in the world, and so please God as you practice true religion.

SERMON NOTES

Bible passage: Date:

SESSION 3:

LOVE: THE HEART OF COMPASSION

"A LIFE WITHOUT LOVE IS LIKE A SUNLESS GARDEN WHEN THE FLOWERS ARE DEAD," SAID THE WRITER OSCAR WILDE. ALL OF US LIKE THE IDEA OF LOVE – BUT IN REALITY, LOVING PEOPLE IS DIFFICULT AND COSTLY. IN THIS SESSION YOU'LL EXPLORE WHAT THE BIBLE SAYS ABOUT WHAT LOVE IS, WHERE IT COMES FROM, AND HOW TO PUT IT INTO PRACTICE.

LOVE: THE HEART OF COMPASSION

Discuss

 1 JOHN 3:11-18

> *¹¹ For this is the message that you have heard from the beginning, that we should love one another. ¹² We should not be like Cain, who was of the evil one and murdered his brother. And why did he murder him? Because his own deeds were evil and his brother's righteous. ¹³ Do not be surprised, brothers, that the world hates you. ¹⁴ We know that we have passed out of death into life, because we love the brothers. Whoever does not love abides in death. ¹⁵ Everyone who hates his brother is a murderer, and you know that no murderer has eternal life abiding in him.*

> *¹⁶ By this we know love, that he laid down his life for us, and we ought to lay down our lives for the brothers. ¹⁷ But if anyone has the world's goods and sees his brother in need, yet closes his heart against him, how does God's love abide in him? ¹⁸ Little children, let us not love in word or talk but in deed and in truth.*

Underline or circle the word "love" every time it occurs in the passage above. Whom does John say we are to love, and how?

_____

_____

_____

_____

_____

_____

_____

_____

▶ **WATCH DVD 3.1 OR LISTEN TO TALK 3.1**

_____

_____

_____

_____

_____

_____

_____

_____

_____

_____

_____

Discuss

"1 John gives us a binary way of seeing the world. People are either 'of the evil one' (v 12) or 'of God.'" How is this contrast seen in the account of Cain and Abel (v 12)?

_____

_____

_____

_____

It is easy to think we are nothing like Cain, but how does verse 15 define a murderer?

_____

_____

_____

_____

▶ **WATCH DVD 3.2 OR LISTEN TO TALK 3.2**

Discuss

Self-sacrifice (v 16): *"By this we know love, that he laid down his life for us, and we ought to lay down our lives for the brothers."*

Most of us will not need to die for the sake of our fellow Christians, though in some circumstances that may be required. How else can you "lay down your life" for others in your church?

Empathy (v 17): *"But if anyone has the world's goods and sees his brother in need, yet closes his heart against him, how does God's love abide in him?"*

When do you find it easy to empathize with the needs of others? When are you at risk of "closing your heart" against them?

Compassion (v 18): *"Little children, let us not love in word or talk but in deed and in truth."*

When do you find yourself talking about fellow believers who need help? What can you do to ensure that your "talk" works itself out "in deed and in truth"?

1 JOHN 3:19-24

[19] By this we shall know that we are of the truth and reassure our heart before him; [20] for whenever our heart condemns us, God is greater than our heart, and he knows everything. [21] Beloved, if our heart does not condemn us, we have confidence before God; [22] and whatever we ask we receive from him, because we keep his commandments and do what pleases him. [23] And this is his commandment, that we believe in the name of his Son Jesus Christ and love one another, just as he has commanded us. [24] Whoever keeps his commandments abides in God, and God in him. And by this we know that he abides in us, by the Spirit whom he has given us.

▶ WATCH DVD 3.3 OR LISTEN TO TALK 3.3

Discuss

"John knows that when we hear the call to a life of love—to empathy, compassion and self-sacrifice—our hearts are going to condemn us as unfeeling, selfish self-pleasers."

How is the gospel both the answer to our self-condemnation and also the spur to love others more fully?

It's easy to get to the end of a session like this thinking, "I must be more loving," but then not do anything about it. Write down three things you can put into practice this week:

1. To show love to someone in your family or a close friend

2. To show love to someone from your church family

3. To show love to someone in your neighborhood

How will you motivate yourself to do these things (v 16)?

Pray

23 And this is his commandment, that we believe in the name of his Son Jesus Christ and love one another, just as he commanded us. 24 Whoever keeps his commandments abides in God, and God in him. And by this we know that he abides in us, by the Spirit whom he has given us." (1 John 3:23-24)

Do you believe in Jesus Christ (v 23)? If so, this faith is a gift from God. Thank him for it.

How much do you love one another (v 23)? Ask God to grow this love in your heart, and to help you work it out in your everyday actions.

Thank God that he abides in you, and you in him (v 24). He has made his home in you; and you have found your home forever in him. Ask him to help you remember this powerful truth as you go about your day, and to more fully reflect his love to others as a result.

DAILY BIBLE DEVOTIONALS

What is love? The devotionals this week will take us through Paul's description in his famous chapter on true love…

Day 1

1 CORINTHIANS 13:1-3

Q: *Imagine a description of a Christian who has done all the things in v 1-3 without the love. How might we look on them?*

Q: *How does God view them?*

"What a wonderful, amazing Christian," we might say, as we read the biographies and look at their achievements in awe. "He was a fantastic preacher, had an amazing mind, achieved astonishing things." "She gave up everything and burned out for the Lord." And yet, God's verdict is very different. *"Nothing. Empty noise. Fruitless."*

This powerful description should give us pause for the way we evaluate others, but also for how we think about our own growth and maturity as a Christian believer. You may be an evangelist, a preacher, a musician, a Bible-study leader or a children's worker; or fulfill some other noble or quiet ministry in the life of your church. But unless you are a lover, you are nothing. You need not a love that just gives you warm feelings in your heart, but a love from Jesus by the Spirit that shapes your relationships, your actions and your priorities.

PRAY: *Jesus, lover of my soul, spare me from being nothing in your eyes. Help me to love others as you love me.*

Day 2

1 CORINTHIANS 13:4

Q: *What makes us impatient, and tempts us to unkindness? Why are these qualities so counterproductive?*

Patience is vital in all human relationships because people can be slow—agonizingly, frustratingly slow. They get on your nerves. They keep making the same mistakes over and over again. Christian love is a thinking love, which actively seeks the best for someone else. It may be that slowness needs a rebuke. But correcting someone in anger or with mockery or sarcasm is a backward step. It may make us feel better to have vented our frustration, but it has not helped the other person at all—it has diminished them.

Q: *Why does genuine Christian love not envy or boast? (See 1 Cor 12:4-6, 11)*

This comes down to recognizing God as the giver of all gifts to us, and to others. He gives his gifts wisely and lovingly—so that we will become more like Jesus, and give him the glory.

PRAY: *Think about times when you have not fitted the picture of love here. Seek God's forgiveness and the strength to grow more loving in these ways today.*

Day 3

1 CORINTHIANS 13:4-5

Q: *How would you feel about spending time with someone who is arrogant, rude, irritable and resentful, and insists on their own way?*

Q: *How have we, by nature, all been this way toward God?*

It's remarkable to reflect on God's love toward us. In the past, we were arrogant—thinking we knew better than God and rejecting his good design for our lives; we were rude—ignoring him, failing to be grateful for all the good things he has given to us; we were irritable and resentful—whenever our conscience pointed to ways we needed to change; and of course, we insisted on our own way—rejecting Jesus' rightful lordship over us. Being with people who treat us like this is utterly unbearable. And yet God loved us still and pursued us in Christ. It is this patient lovingkindness that God has shown to us that we are called on to show to others.

How we treat even the "little people" around us will show how much we have understood the gospel; and it will allow others to glimpse the love of God for them, through us.

Q: *Is there anyone you need to apologize to? Resolve to do it today.*

PRAY: *Thank you, Father, that you loved me even when I was so horribly arrogant before you. Please help me to show to others the love you have shown to me.*

Day 4

1 CORINTHIANS 13:6

Q: *When might we be tempted to rejoice at wrongdoing?*

Q: *When might we be tempted not to rejoice over the truth?*

The Corinthians had become so obsessed with their freedom in Christ that they had lost sight of God's holiness and guidance on what is good and right and leads to our flourishing. They were celebrating things that were clearly contrary to God's law and will. And Paul connects such moral matters directly to love. He is saying that it is simply unloving to suggest to people that doing wrong is fine. There is always a price to pay when we divert from God's pattern for living.

The same is true of false teaching. Bad theology is not just wrong thinking—it is cruel and enslaving, and therefore *unloving* of us to allow it to go unchallenged. Sound teaching is healthy and life-giving; it leads to our liberation and fulfillment in Christ, which is why love rejoices over the truth—even when it is a hard truth for us to hear.

Q: *Are you allowing the truth to set you free—even the hard truths that you would rather not hear?*

PRAY: *Help me, Lord, to rejoice over the truth wherever I hear it, and to commend its goodness to others.*

Day 5

1 CORINTHIANS 13:7

Have you ever given up on a friendship with someone because it was just too difficult?

Q: *What are the "things" that love believes and hopes for?*

Q: *What is the connection between belief and hope, and the ability to bear trials and endure?*

Perhaps Paul has in mind the selective beliefs of the Corinthian church—picking and choosing the things that made them feel good, but rejecting the parts of God's word that were less palatable. When we do that, we can enjoy a version of the Christian life that will, however, utterly fail us when suffering or difficulties come—which they inevitably will. When we grasp the whole counsel of God, it enables us to endure, because we see that God is working in all things to make us more like Christ. When our hope is properly centered on the world to come, we can keep going in adversity because, like a runner in a race, we can see the finishing line up ahead.

The point is that love informed by such faith and hope simply does not quit. It does not give up, even when faced with massive discouragement, opposition or persecution. Our love for others and for the Lord is shaped and energized by a deeper understanding of who God is, where we are now, and what our destiny will be.

PRAY: *Talk to the Lord about some people whom you have found too hard to persevere with; people you have given up praying for, perhaps.*

Day 6

1 CORINTHIANS 13:8

Our culture says that love is a feeling; it ebbs and flows, and sometimes it fails. But God shows that love is more of a decision than an emotion. It is a conscious commitment to do what is best for someone else, no matter how hard, and no matter what they do. This is the kind of love that God has for us, and will always have for us. It "never ends."

Q: *Why does it make all the difference that your love for someone is not to be based on your emotions, but on your decisions?*

We easily give in to an "if I feel like it" culture. That is not godly love at all. Gethsemane shows us that Jesus did not particularly "feel like" going to the cross. But he sought his Father's help to endure and follow through on his decision to love us to the end.

1 CORINTHIANS 13:8-13

Q: *What is truly important in this life? What is truly important in eternity? Why the difference?*

Think of some people whom you love (and perhaps those whom you struggle to love well). Read through 1 Corinthians 13 v 4-7, and consider how Jesus has loved you perfectly in these ways. Now think through how you can love others with a more Christ-like love.

PRAY: *Spend time thanking Jesus that he loved you with an enduring love that took him to the cross. Ask the Father to strengthen you by the Spirit to love others as Jesus loved you.*

 **JOURNAL**

What I've learned or been particularly struck by this week…

What I want to change in my perspectives or actions as a resul

Things I would like to think about more or discuss with others at

BIBLE STUDY

Discuss

"How can you tell if someone really loves you?" How do you think most people would answer this question?

👉 **READ 1 JOHN 4:7-21**

[7] Beloved, let us love one another, for love is from God, and whoever loves has been born of God and knows God. [8] Anyone who does not love does not know God, because God is love. [9] In this the love of God was made manifest among us, that God sent his only Son into the world, so that we might live through him.

1. *Why* should we love one another (v 7-12)?

2. *How* should we love one another?

What does the cross reveal about God's love?

3. What amazing claim is made in verse 12?

_____

_____

_____

What implications does this have for our outreach and pastoral care as a church?

_____

_____

_____

_____

_____

4. How can we know for sure that we are a genuine Christian (v 13-16)? Is it possible to tell if someone else is a genuine believer? Why / Why not?

_____

_____

_____

_____

Is love for others or belief in the truth the most important sign that someone follows correct teaching? How are the two connected?

_____

_____

_____

_____

5. Where does genuine Christian love come from (v 19)? How can we grow in that love?

How can love be commanded (v 21)? What are the implications for how we seek to grow our love?

Summarize

How would you answer Question 1 after thinking about this passage? How would you answer the question: How can you tell that someone loves Jesus?

Apply

FOR YOURSELF AND YOUR CHURCH: Who do you find difficult to love, both as individuals and corporately as a church? How can you encourage each other to be more loving, both in quantity and quality?

Pray

FOR YOUR GROUP: Pray that you would understand God's love for you in Christ more deeply than ever. Pray that your love would be suffused with the knowledge and wisdom of Christ, as you reflect on his word.

FOR YOUR CHURCH: Pray that your love for each other would spill over into the world, and that those who spend time with you would see Jesus in your life, as you love others selflessly and with generosity.

SERMON NOTES

Bible passage: Date:

SESSION 4:

MERCY: HEARTS
MADE SOFT

SO FAR WE'VE DISCOVERED THAT GOD DESIRES A WORLD
OF SHALOM; WE'VE SEEN HOW GOD CALLS HIS PEOPLE
TO WORK FOR JUSTICE; AND WE'VE BEEN CHALLENGED
TO LIVE A LIFE CHARACTERIZED BY SELF-GIVING LOVE.
IN THIS SESSION WE'LL TIE ALL THOSE IDEAS TOGETHER
AS WE LOOK AT THE THEME OF MERCY – AND REFRESH
OURSELVES IN THE FOUNTAIN OF MERCY: JESUS CHRIST.

MERCY: HEARTS MADE SOFT

Discuss

Imagine if we started this session by asking each person to tell the group who they have shown mercy to in the last week. Would you want to answer the question? Why / why not?

_____

_____

_____

_____

_____

▶ WATCH DVD 4.1 OR LISTEN TO TALK 4.1

_____

_____

_____

_____

_____

_____

_____

_____

_____

_____

MATTHEW 25:31-46

³¹ "When the Son of Man comes in his glory, and all the angels with him, then he will sit on his glorious throne. ³² Before him will be gathered all the nations, and he will separate people one from another as a shepherd separates the sheep from the goats. ³³ And he will place the sheep on his right, but the goats on the left. ³⁴ Then the King will say to those on his right, 'Come, you who are blessed by my Father, inherit the kingdom prepared for you from the foundation of the world. ³⁵ For I was hungry and you gave me food, I was thirsty and you gave me drink, I was a stranger and you welcomed me, ³⁶ I was naked and you clothed me, I was sick and you visited me, I was in prison and you came to me.' ³⁷ Then the righteous will answer him, saying, 'Lord, when did we see you hungry and feed you, or thirsty and give you drink? ³⁸ And when did we see you a stranger and welcome you, or naked and clothe you? ³⁹ And when did we see you sick or in prison and visit you?' ⁴⁰ And the King will answer them, 'Truly, I say to you, as you did it to one of the least of these my brothers, you did it to me.'

⁴¹ "Then he will say to those on his left, 'Depart from me, you cursed, into the eternal fire prepared for the devil and his angels. ⁴² For I was hungry and you gave me no food, I was thirsty and you gave me no drink, ⁴³ I was a stranger and you did not welcome me, naked and you did not clothe me, sick and in prison and you did not visit me.' ⁴⁴ Then they also will answer, saying, 'Lord, when did we see you hungry or thirsty or a stranger or naked or sick or in prison, and did not minister to you?' ⁴⁵ Then he will answer them, saying, 'Truly, I say to you, as you did not do it to one of the least of these, you did not do it to me.' ⁴⁶ And these will go away into eternal punishment, but the righteous into eternal life."

Discuss

This session builds on the details in Jesus' account of the sheep and the goats in Matthew 25:31-46. Use these verses to fill in the table opposite.

	Sheep	Goats
Where will Jesus put people (v 33)?		
How does Jesus describe them?	v 34:	v 41:
Where will they go?	v 34: v 46:	v 41: v 46:
What did they do / not do for Jesus?	v 35 (3 things): v 36 (3 things):	v 42 (2 things): v 43 (4 things):

When is this separation going to occur (v 31)?

_____

_____

_____

▶ **WATCH DVD 4.2 OR LISTEN TO TALK 4.2**

Discuss

Does Jesus list people's acts of mercy before or after he separates them into sheep and goats? Why does this matter?

Who are the sheep being merciful to (v 40)? Is that who you expected Jesus to be talking about?

"Mercy is the mark of a church that has been shaped by the gospel." If someone came to visit your church or group for the first time, or found out about it some other way (e.g. asking around, checking out your website), would they say it is marked by mercy? How would they know? What about someone who lives in the neighborhood, but isn't a member of the church? Would their view be different?

▶ **WATCH DVD 4.3 OR LISTEN TO TALK 4.3**

Discuss

Look at your list on page 77 of the kinds of acts of mercy the sheep were doing. Which of these are you currently involved in, either as individuals or as a church? How could you add the others?

_____

_____

_____

_____

_____

What changes are you going to make as a result of this session?

_____

_____

_____

_____

_____

Pray

"Jesus, the Good Shepherd, became a sheep and was slaughtered for us.
- *Because he went hungry, we are fed with the bread of life.*
- *Because he went thirsty, we drink living water.*
- *Because he became a stranger, we experience welcome.*
- *Because he was stripped naked, we are clothed with robes of righteousness.*
- *Because he was executed as a criminal, we are set free.*
- *Because he bore death, we experience life."*

Turn each of the points above into a prayer of thankfulness to Jesus, our Good Shepherd.

Now look at the action points you have listed above, and ask God to help you start to make them a reality this week.

DAILY BIBLE DEVOTIONALS

Mercy is love in action for those in need. In the devotionals this week, we'll look slowly and carefully at the famous story Jesus told about a Samaritan…

Day 1

LUKE 10:25-28

Q: *What does the lawyer ask Jesus? What is he hoping to gain from his question?*

He stands up to test Jesus, perhaps thinking the Lord will make some outrageous statement that could be used against him. But Jesus seems to play it straight: *You're a lawyer—what does the law say?*

Q: *Read the words of v 27 again, slowly. If this is the way to inherit eternal life, how do these commands make you feel?*

Q: *What is the implied challenge in Jesus' comment of verse 28?*

His statement to go and do it is a provocative challenge to the basis for any rule-keeping religion. *You've got it right: now live it!* But the question hangs in the air: how can anyone really, truly say that they have met this requirement—total all-consuming love for God and complete and selfless love for neighbor? It's a challenge that, without the gospel, can only force us into self-deception or leave us on our knees in despair.

Q: *Which of these responses is most "you"?*

PRAY: *Lord, show me more deeply the extent of your holy law, and the depth of my failure to keep it.*

Day 2

LUKE 10:29

Q: *What is so sad about verse 29?*

Q: *What would your answer to the question be if you did not know what follows?*

Jesus' answer was designed to reveal the huge gap between our performance and perfection. It should have led the lawyer to seek God's grace and mercy to justify him. Instead he opts for one of the classic techniques of law-keeping religion. Some fool themselves (but not others) that they are, in fact, keeping the law—but he tries to shrink the requirements of the law, so that he can justify *himself*. That is the ultimate tragedy of rule-based religion. We attempt to justify ourselves, by hard work, obsessive attention to detail, or by recasting the law to fit our own preferences. None of these work. The ultimate tragedy of the lawyer's statement is that he seeks to justify himself to the only person who can ultimately justify him through his death on the cross.

Q: *How can you fight against your instinct to rely on rule-based religion?*

PRAY: *Lord, show me where I am prone to justifying myself before you, and help me to see your greater provision for my forgiveness through Jesus. Amen.*

Day 3

Q: *Why does Jesus answer with a story?*

LUKE 10:29-32

Stories can be so effective at answering people who are locked into a wrong way of thinking. Think of the prophet Nathan with David (2 Sam 12). Jesus is speaking to a man from the Jewish religious establishment, whose whole life has been consumed with studying and thinking about the law of God. But his only way to keep it is to "shrink to fit." Jesus' story takes him away from academic debate to a real person, with a real need, who is desperate for some practical love to be shown to him.

Q: *How might the priest and the Levite have "justified themselves" in walking by?*

Q: *How might you?*

There's always a great reason not to show practical love and compassion to others. We're too busy; it's too dangerous; there's a different/higher calling on my time. Perhaps the worst thing is when we somehow "spiritualize" our lack of compassion, convincing ourselves that God is more pleased with us passing by on the other side.

One clue to the meaning is in the wording of the command. "Love your neighbor *as yourself.*" It is caught up in Jesus' Golden Rule: "And as you wish that others would do to you, do so to them" (Luke 6:31).

PRAY: *Lord, help me not to be someone who passes by on the other side. Help me to respond to my neighbor's need with your loving compassion. Amen.*

Day 4

After the priest and the Levite, what might the hearers be expecting as the punchline? Perhaps the questioner was expecting Jesus to say, "But a lawyer…"!

LUKE 10:33

Q: *Why would this sentence be such a shock to those listening?*

Q: *If Jesus was telling this story today, what characters might he have chosen to include?*

Samaritans were hated, racially impure, theologically off-track, and despised as inferior in every way. And yet, the key point is that, unlike the sound, racially pure, in-every-way-superior priest and Levite, he "*had compassion.*" They had none.

Q: *How are loving God and loving our neighbor interconnected? How can we set these commands against each other?*

Loving our neighbor is not an add-on. In many ways it is part of the visible proof that we are loving God with all our heart, mind, soul and strength. We can easily elevate loving others practically over our worship, doctrine and evangelism, and vice versa. But both are intertwined. We cannot be loving God if we have no compassion for others. And genuine Christian compassion for others must be informed and driven by a love for the Lord.

PRAY: *Lord, give me a heart of compassion for the wounded, bruised and needy of this world. Help me to love others as you have loved me in Christ. Amen.*

Day 5

LUKE 10:34-35

Q: *What can we learn about godly love of neighbor from the details of this story?*

Q: *How is this a challenge to our own view of how we should love our neighbor?*

The Samaritan cares for an unknown man from a country and race that is hostile to him. He simply responds to the need. Notice that he is also extremely diligent in how he cares for him. He binds his wounds with what medicine he has available—oil and wine. He transports him at cost to himself—he walks while the man is carried on his steed. He cares for him through the night at the inn, and then gives to meet his need while he recovers, making full provision for his recovery by his promise to repay whatever is spent on him. He is meticulous. He is thorough. He is thoughtful. His focus is on the restoration of the stranger and not on what it costs him, or the inconvenience to his time and plans.

You might already be trying to work out how to "justify yourself" for adopting a standard lower than the Samaritan's. Of course, there are limits to what we can give, the energy we have, or the number of people we can help. But before any of that, let's focus clearly on the level and kind of compassion we are called to.

Q: *Think about one person you can show compassion to today. How will you be thoughtful, thorough and sacrificial?*

PRAY: *Lord, please give me your heart of compassion for the lost and needy. Help me to care practically and responsibly for those you guide me to. Amen.*

Day 6

LUKE 10:36-37

Q: *How does Jesus' story answer the lawyer's original question in v 29?*

The lawyer has asked, "Who is my neighbor?" (v 29). But Jesus says, *Wrong question!* Instead, the story about the Samaritan flips the question on its head. Not "Who is my neighbor?" but "How can I be a neighbor?"

The most obvious answer to the lawyer's question is that your neighbor is *anyone* whom you come across that you can give help to—whatever their situation, their status or their nationality. That's an enormous challenge for us in our highly connected world, where we have a huge range of possibilities for giving, serving and helping.

Many Christians plan their giving to charitable causes involved in international relief, medical research or poverty relief. But even as we plan such consistent compassion, we should not think that absolves us from personally reacting to the suffering and need we come across in our day-to-day lives, or from giving particular help in emergencies, like a famine, war, or natural disaster. Jesus calls his followers to have compassionate hearts that are eager to give of themselves, not counting the cost, because we see a need that we can help with.

Q: *How much room do you allow in your life for spontaneous opportunities to love?*

PRAY: *Lord, thank you for the way this story convicts us of our lack of love and compassion for others. Please help me to give my money, my time, myself to those in need—for Jesus' sake. Amen.*

JOURNAL

What I've learned or been particularly struck by this week…

What I want to change in my perspectives or actions as a result of this week…

Things I would like to think about more or discuss with others at my church…

BIBLE STUDY

Discuss

Many churches struggle to work out how much energy to put into "mercy ministries" they may be involved in, as opposed to evangelism. This is not a new problem, as will be seen in this study on the early church.

Do you think your church is taking practical mercy and gospel evangelism seriously? Make a quick list of what your church does in each area. Do you think this is a healthy balance, or are you concerned that one is detracting from the other?

☛ READ ACTS 6:1-7

¹ Now in these days when the disciples were increasing in number, a complaint by the Hellenists arose against the Hebrews because their widows were being neglected in the daily distribution.

1. What was the practice of the early church in regard to the needy?

What situation had arisen? Why was it potentially so damaging?

2. What was the apostles' solution? What wrong steps could they have taken instead?

What is distinctive about the people they chose? What lessons are there in this for us?

3. What was the result of this change (v 7)? How did that happen?

👉 **SCAN-READ ACTS 6:7 – 7:60**

> [8] And Stephen, full of grace and power, was doing great wonders and signs among the people. [9] Then some of those who belonged to the synagogue of the Freedmen (as it was called), and of the Cyrenians, and of the Alexandrians, and of those from Cilicia and Asia, rose up and disputed with Stephen.

4. What happened next? Why is it important for us to remember this?

_____

_____

_____

_____

_____

Apply

FOR YOUR CHURCH: Revisit the opening discussion question in light of what you have read in Acts. Is your answer still the same? How would you go about doing something to change it?

_____

_____

_____

_____

_____

Pray

FOR YOUR CHURCH: Pray that you would discharge your responsibilities as a congregation to care for the needy in your church, and those in your wider community.

FOR YOUR COMMUNITY: Pray for gospel growth in and through your church, and for people to become genuine Christians.

FOR YOUR LEADERS: Pray for those who give themselves to preaching and prayer; and for those who give themselves to mercy ministries—that they would all be filled with the Spirit to do the work God has called them to.

SERMON NOTES

Bible passage: Date:

SESSION 5:

GENEROSITY: STEWARDING GOD'S MONEY

THIS SESSION IS ABOUT MONEY. FOR MOST OF US, IT'S A TOPIC WE'D RATHER NOT TALK ABOUT PUBLICLY. BUT FOR THE BIBLE-WRITER JAMES, IT'S A TOPIC HE TACKLES HEAD ON. IN THIS SESSION WE'LL BE CHALLENGED BY SOME UNCOMFORTABLE TRUTHS – BUT WE'LL ALSO BE WOWED BY GOD'S OVERFLOWING GENEROSITY.

GENEROSITY: STEWARDING GOD'S MONEY

Discuss

This session digs into various parts of the letter of James. Who was James writing to? (See James 1:1.)

How does he describe his readers in chapter 1? (See verses 2, 16 and 19.)

▶ WATCH DVD 5.1 OR LISTEN TO TALK 5.1

👉 JAMES 2:1-10

¹ My brothers, show no partiality as you hold the faith in our Lord Jesus Christ, the Lord of glory. ² For if a man wearing a gold ring and fine clothing comes into your assembly, and a poor man in shabby clothing also comes in, ³ and if you pay attention to the one who wears the fine clothing and say, "You sit here in a good place," while you say to the poor man, "You stand over there," or, "Sit down at my feet," ⁴ have you not then made distinctions among yourselves and become judges with evil thoughts? ⁵ Listen, my beloved brothers, has not God chosen those who are poor in the world to be rich in faith and heirs of the kingdom, which he has promised to those who love him? ⁶ But you have dishonored the poor man. Are not the rich the ones who oppress you, and the ones who drag you into court? ⁷ Are they not the ones who blaspheme the honorable name by which you were called?

⁸ If you really fulfill the royal law according to the Scripture, "You shall love your neighbor as yourself," you are doing well. ⁹ But if you show partiality, you are committing sin and are convicted by the law as transgressors. ¹⁰ For whoever keeps the whole law but fails in one point has become accountable for all of it.

Discuss

Do you agree that money is "the elephant in the room" (or, perhaps, "the elephant in the church"!)? Why do you think that is?

_____

_____

_____

_____

JAMES 1:9-11

⁹ Let the lowly brother boast in his exaltation, ¹⁰ and the rich in his humiliation, because like a flower of the grass he will pass away. ¹¹ For the sun rises with its scorching heat and withers the grass; its flower falls, and its beauty perishes. So also will the rich man fade away in the midst of his pursuits.

What do we learn about the rich in these verses?

_____

_____

_____

👉 JAMES 1:16-18

16 Do not be deceived, my beloved brothers. 17 Every good gift and every perfect gift is from above, coming down from the Father of lights, with whom there is no variation or shadow due to change. 18 Of his own will he brought us forth by the word of truth, that we should be a kind of firstfruits of his creatures.

What do verses 16-18 tell us about God?

_____

_____

_____

_____

Bearing in mind what God is like, let's think about money. If our money is a gift from God (v 17), how does that make you feel about a) your money, b) the things you have bought with your money, c) the ways you could spend your money?

_____

_____

_____

_____

_____

_____

_____

▶ WATCH DVD 5.2 OR LISTEN TO TALK 5.2

_____

JAMES 5:1-6

¹ Come now, you rich, weep and howl for the miseries that are coming upon you. ² Your riches have rotted and your garments are moth-eaten. ³ Your gold and silver have corroded, and their corrosion will be evidence against you and will eat your flesh like fire. You have laid up treasure in the last days. ⁴ Behold, the wages of the laborers who mowed your fields, which you kept back by fraud, are crying out against you, and the cries of the harvesters have reached the ears of the Lord of hosts. ⁵ You have lived on the earth in luxury and in self-indulgence. You have fattened your hearts in a day of slaughter. ⁶ You have condemned and murdered the righteous person. He does not resist you.

Discuss

What does James accuse these rich people of doing?

_____

_____

_____

It's easy to assume that we would never do these things, but what are the heart attitudes behind their actions?

_____

_____

_____

It is very easy for us to treat wealth in an ungodly way. As you think about your money and possessions, when might you be tempted to show similar wrong attitudes in your heart?

_____

_____

_____

_____

_____

_____

▶ **WATCH DVD 5.3 OR LISTEN TO TALK 5.3**

_____

_____

_____

_____

_____

_____

_____

_____

_____

_____

_____

Discuss

"God does not hoard his riches—he freely gives them away. God does not defraud—he goes above and beyond and gives his very self. God is not self-indulgent—in the gospel he engages in self-deprivation for the good of others."

Think about any tendency you may have to be a hoarder or compulsive consumer. How will God's example help you to change?

Instead of being tempted toward fraud/injustice, how can you make God's giving of himself a pattern to follow for your own giving, even to the point where it hurts?

"Self-indulgence is counter to our identity in Christ." How will the self-deprivation of Jesus help you to fight the temptation in your own heart to indulge yourself?

What are you going to change as a result of this session?

Pray

Look again at your list of God's characteristics on page 97. Taking each one in turn, thank him for this aspect of his goodness and ask him to help you live as his image-bearers.

DAILY BIBLE DEVOTIONALS

We may find it difficult to talk about money, but Jesus didn't. This week's devotionals look at a saying from the Gospels on money each day, with a proverb to pray...

Day 1

MATTHEW 5:42

Q: *What questions and objections spring into your mind as soon as you read this verse?*

Q: *Why do we find these words of Jesus so hard to hear?*

We might excuse ourselves by thinking that we want to use our money with wisdom. Would we give to someone in the street who we suspect will spend the money on drugs? Would we lend to someone who we think will not use the money sensibly or carefully? I suspect Jesus puts his command as starkly as he does because he knows our hearts. The power and pull of money on us is immensely strong. To break it, he calls us to embrace a kind of carelessness about money that will overwhelm our temptation to disguise our own love for money as "wisdom." Sometimes, even if we suspect the money will not be well used, it will be good for us just to give, so that our hearts are turned to God instead of mammon.

PRAY: *Proverbs 3:27. Do not withhold good from those who deserve it, when it's in your power to help them.*

Day 2

Q: *How would you advise a child or a student or a cash-strapped family about their giving?*

We might advise them in two ways. "Don't give now. Save your money; leave it until you have a good job; take care of yourself first, and then see what you have left over to give." Or "pay the God tax" of 10 per cent.

MARK 12:41-44

Q: *How does God measure the value of our giving?*

Q: *Having read the story about the widow, how might you change your advice?*

It's not what you give, but how it expresses your dependence on God. It's not how much you give, but how sacrificial it is. The woman gave a pathetic sum, but it was all she had to live on; that's why Jesus commended her. And it's the reason why we should all make generous giving part of our lives, whatever our situation. If we develop a habit of generosity, we will close the door to money's grip on us; and make our focus God's provision for us.

PRAY: *Proverbs 1:18-19. Self-destruction is the fate of all who are greedy for money; it robs them of life.*

Day 3

LUKE 3:14

Soldiering, like tax collecting, involved living off the people you were supposedly protecting. It may be self-evidently wrong to our modern minds, but it was just "how the world works" to them. So John's answer to their question is both shocking and radical.

Q: *What principles does he lay out?*

Q: *In what subtle ways can we be doing the same things today?*

If you are running an extortion racket and reading this, please stop immediately! But how might we top up our income in ways that may not please God? It's easy to do "little jobs" for cash, and not declare them for tax—in effect we are cheating our government, and, in turn, the poor and needy who rely on payments and services they receive. We do the same thing when we collude with workers who want to be paid in cash.

The bite comes for us in the last phrase: "Be content with your wages." That doesn't mean that we should not ask for a pay raise or seek a better job. But it does mean that we should be more concerned about pleasing God than gaining extra money. If we have truly repented, then there will be some evidence of it on our bank statement.

PRAY: *Proverbs 15:6. There is treasure in the house of the godly, but the earnings of the wicked bring trouble.*

Day 4

MATTHEW 6:19-21

These verses perhaps best summarize Jesus' teaching about money. Read the words, slowly, carefully and prayerfully…

Q: *What is at stake in our attitude toward money?*

Q: *What test does Jesus offer us to assess where we are on this issue? How might you apply that to yourself?*

Eternity is at stake. If we have a bigger perspective than this life, we will immediately see how pointless it is to expend our energies on amassing wealth. "You can't take it with you." "There are no pockets in a shroud." But it is worse than pointless—it's *deadly.* When our hearts are set on earthly wealth, they are turned away from the only wealth that really matters. We might test ourselves by monitoring our instincts about money and wealth. Do we dream of exotic holidays, or the latest piece of tech, or a new kitchen, or a larger house? Or do we dream about unconverted friends brought to the foot of the cross, or the gospel brought to hostile and remote corners of the earth, or the comfort and hope brought to the poor and needy through a mercy ministry we might start? Which of these puts a smile on your face?

Q: *How exactly can you "lay up treasure in heaven" for yourself today?*

PRAY: *Proverbs 23:5. In the blink of an eye wealth disappears, for it will sprout wings and fly away like an eagle.*

Day 5

LUKE 16:13

Q: *How might we be tempted to get around this bold binary statement?*

The Lord Jesus leaves us no "wriggle room" at all in this sharp and uncompromising summary. We can be very creative in the ways we obscure our love for money in order to escape the full blast of Jesus statement: "You *cannot* serve God and money." "It's not that I exactly *love* money. It's not that I exactly *hate* God. I like what money buys me…" But the Lord directly connects the two. What you give to one cannot be given to the other. It's not just that a little love of money means that I love God a little less. Jesus tells us that *any* attachment to wealth will negate our love for God. He gives us a stark either/or choice.

Q: *How can we stop serving money?*

God is jealous for our hearts. When we worship money, we are worshiping the gift and not the Giver. A first step might be to stop fooling ourselves over whether it really matters: it does. A second step might be to understand how generous God really is, and how he owns both us and all the possessions we have. Reminding ourselves that it is the Lord's money in our bank account and pocket, and it is the Lord's house that I live in, and his car that I drive, might be the start of a quiet revolution…

PRAY: *Proverbs 11:28. Trust in your money and down you go! But the godly flourish like leaves in spring.*

Day 6

MATTHEW 6:25-34

Q: *What is anxiety a sign of (v 30)?*

Q: *What is the cure for this kind of anxiety, according to Jesus?*

Q: *What are "all these things" that will be added to us as we trust God (v 33)?*

Jesus was speaking into a culture where even having something to eat or wear was the reason for anxiety. We tend to elevate our anxiety to a much more refined, and trivial level. "Does this outfit work?" "Do these shoes match?" "Will I make the right impression?" "What will we cook for the smart dinner party we are organizing?"

The cure to our anxieties is to understand that "your heavenly Father knows that you need them all" (v 32). That we trust in a Father who provides for our needs, not our wants. That we look to him for our sense of what truly matters, and even what is beautiful.

We need to drag our eyes away from the mirror and the menu, and focus them on the Master and his mission: the kingdom of God.

Q: *What does v 34 add to the picture?*

We're not promised that all will be sweetness and light—there will be "troubles." But a day-by-day dependence on a loving Father who provides for us is the key to an anxiety-free life.

PRAY: *Proverbs 10:22. The blessing of the LORD makes a person rich, and he adds no sorrow with it.*

JOURNAL

What I've learned or been particularly struck by this week…

What I want to change in my perspectives or actions as a result of this week…

Things I would like to think about more or discuss with others at my church…

BIBLE STUDY

Discuss

When someone talks about money, giving or special collections, what are some reactions that go on inside our heads? Why?

READ 2 CORINTHIANS 8:1-15

¹ We want you to know, brothers, about the grace of God that has been given among the churches of Macedonia, ² for in a severe test of affliction, their abundance of joy and their extreme poverty have overflowed in a wealth of generosity on their part. ³ For they gave according to their means, as I can testify, and beyond their means, of their own accord...

1. What is remarkable about the giving of the Macedonian churches?

_____

_____

_____

_____

_____

Where does this come from? How is it described?

_____

_____

_____

_____

2. How did the Macedonians view their giving?

How is this attitude toward giving in conflict with our culture's view of wealth?

3. How is this a challenge to the Corinthian church (v 7)?

In what ways might we have a similar attitude to the Corinthians?

4. Does Paul command them to give? What motive is he looking for (v 7-9)?

What makes a gift "acceptable" (v 9-14)? How will that involve our head (what we think), our heart (what we feel), and our hands (what we do)?

5. What does the picture in verse 15 add to our understanding of generosity?

Apply

FOR YOURSELF: How does the giving described here compare with your own thinking about money and giving?

Pray

FOR YOURSELF: Ask God to give you "the grace of giving" as you reflect on the Lord Jesus who gave up "sapphire-paved courts for stable floor." Pray that you would be eager, willing and practical in your approach to giving in the future.

FOR YOUR CHURCH: Ask God to make you generous like your Macedonian brothers and sisters of old.

SERMON NOTES

Bible passage: Date:

SESSION 6:

RECONCILIATION: RELATIONSHIPS HEALED

PART OF LIVING IN A WORLD THIS SIDE OF SHALOM IS THE REALITY OF BROKEN RELATIONSHIPS. THE FRIEND WE'VE GIVEN THE COLD SHOULDER TO; THE FAMILY MEMBER WE HARBOR A BITTERNESS AGAINST; THE ARGUMENT OVER WHICH WE'VE NEVER MADE UP. IS THERE ANY HOPE FOR OUR RELATIONAL MESSES? THIS SESSION, WE'LL FOCUS IN ON JUST ONE WORD: RECONCILIATION.

RECONCILIATION: RELATIONSHIPS HEALED

Discuss

How would you define "reconciliation," using a maximum of six words?

_____

_____

_____

▶ WATCH DVD 6.1 OR LISTEN TO TALK 6.1

_____

_____

_____

_____

_____

_____

_____

_____

_____

_____

_____

Discuss

This session is based on some of Jesus' teaching from the Sermon on the Mount (Matthew 5 – 7). Who was Jesus teaching? (See Matthew 5:1-2.) But who else was listening? (See Matthew 7:28-29.)

What are we to do with Jesus' teaching in the Sermon on the Mount? Read Matthew 7:24 and compare with 7:26.

👉 MATTHEW 5:21-26

21 You have heard that it was said to those of old, "You shall not murder; and whoever murders will be liable to judgment." 22 But I say to you that everyone who is angry with his brother will be liable to judgment; whoever insults his brother will be liable to the council; and whoever says, "You fool!" will be liable to the hell of fire. 23 So if you are offering your gift at the altar and there remember that your brother has something against you, 24 leave your gift there before the altar and go. First be reconciled to your brother, and then come and offer your gift. 25 Come to terms quickly with your accuser while you are going with him to court, lest your accuser hand you over to the judge, and the judge to the guard, and you be put in prison. 26 Truly, I say to you, you will never get out until you have paid the last penny.

▶ **WATCH DVD 6.2 OR LISTEN TO TALK 6.2**

Discuss

The sixth of the Ten Commandments says, "You shall not murder" (Exodus 20:13). In Matthew 5:22, what does Jesus say is the equivalent to murder?

At first glance, it could look as if Jesus lists these examples so that, as long as we avoid all of them, we can be sure we don't accidentally break the sixth commandment. But what deeper heart issue is Jesus revealing here?

Reconciliation is at the heart of the Christian faith, as shown by our need for a Savior who can reconcile us to God. Jesus speaks, here, about the need to be reconciled with our fellow Christians. How do we know from these verses that this kind of reconciliation is important to God? Why do you think this is?

In these verses, we see that failing to seek reconciliation is the equivalent of murder in the eyes of God. What does Jesus say we are to do if/when we remember that we are not reconciled with someone else? Are these instructions for all Christians, or for those God has especially chosen to be peacemakers?

▶ **WATCH DVD 6.3 OR LISTEN TO TALK 6.3**

COLOSSIANS 1:19-20

19 For in him all the fullness of God was pleased to dwell, 20 and through him to reconcile to himself all things, whether on earth or in heaven, making peace by the blood of his cross.

Discuss

"The practice of reconciliation is simply the act of re-gifting what you have received to someone else." Think about the following scenarios. How could you, either as individuals or as a church family, "re-gift" the reconciliation you have received in these situations?

- As you are dropping your child at school, you see two mothers having an argument. How could you act as a peacemaker in this situation?

- In the last year, a couple have left your church because they were unhappy with the style of music. What would it look like to reach out to them—not necessarily to try and bring them back into your church family, but to be reconciled with them?

- A long-standing member of your church family has recently died. At the funeral, her two sons, also church members, start arguing over which of them should inherit a valuable painting. How can you help them to be reconciled?

These scenarios were invented. But how can you apply your answers to them to current situations facing you, either as individuals or within the church?

_____

_____

_____

_____

_____

_____

Pray

"Jesus opened up the cosmic filing cabinet, pulled out our record of law-breaking, and replaced it with his perfect record of law-keeping."

Spend some time praising and thanking Jesus for making it possible for us to be reconciled to God through his death and resurrection.

Think about anyone with whom you need to be reconciled. Confess to God your part in the breakdown of that relationship. Ask him to help you to obey Jesus' words by going to that person and doing whatever rightly needs to be done to be reconciled with them.

Pray for those you know who have a wider role as peacemakers—maybe your church leaders, those working in the local community, or those in wider government. Ask God to give them wisdom and grace as they seek to bring people back together.

DAILY BIBLE DEVOTIONALS

We are called to be reconciled with one another and united as believers. These readings will help us see both the opportunity and challenge of our calling to be peacemakers.

Day 1

EPHESIANS 2:17-22

There was a barrier between Jews and Gentiles—quite literally—in the Jerusalem Temple. Paul has been showing how Jesus removes that barrier and brings together two hostile and alienated groups.

Q: *What pictures does Paul use to illustrate how Christ unites everyone?*

Q: *How does the tense of verse 22 help us understand what we need to work at?*

Close, not distant; one nation, not two; members of the same household; built on the same foundations; a new, united temple. Paul stacks up the Bible-rich pictures to make his point. Through grace, we are all brought near to God and one another. It's a joy to those who were once excluded, but a struggle perhaps for those who thought they were "special." Our unity is a fact—we *are* one in Christ. But we are in the process of *being built*. It will be a lifelong struggle to make this a reality.

Q: *How can you work to make our unity in Christ more real for you, and for others?*

PRAY: *Lord, thank you that in Christ, we are all one. Help me realize that vision for myself and my church community.*

Day 2

How do we grow in our unity as believers?

COLOSSIANS 3:12-15

Q: *How does the knowledge that we are chosen, holy, and loved help us deal differently with the things that threaten to push us apart, do you think?*

Q: *What else is needed to realize this unity among those who belong to Christ?*

When we disagree with one another, or if there is a personality clash, our tendency is to find our security and significance in the fact that we are right and others are wrong. We look for love and acceptance from the group that supports our case against our opponent. But the gospel teaches us that we share our security and significance together in our status as God's children: we are all loved and called to live holy lives. And it is that Spirit-empowered, Jesus-like character we need to deal with our sinful tendencies to fly apart from each other. The ability to forgive each other is only possible when we see how much we have been forgiven.

Q: *Which of the qualities in verse 12 do you particularly need to grow in?*

PRAY: *Father, help me to forgive and love others as you have forgiven and love me.*

Day 3

GENESIS 45:1-5

The climax of the story of Joseph, Pharaoh, famines and family is this emotional reconciliation between the once-estranged brothers.

Q: *How do the brothers react? What are they fearful of?*

Q: *Why does Joseph see things differently?*

Previously, Joseph's brothers would have been quite happy to kill him (see Genesis 37:4-5). Now they are justifiably fearful that their brother will take revenge. But Joseph's experience has not made him bitter; it has taught him to see things differently. There is a sovereign God who orders the world so that his purposes are fulfilled. When we are hostile to someone or angry with them, the emotions are all we can see—they overwhelm us. But Joseph sets all believers a wonderful example. He is able to distance himself from the hurt he feels and the justified anger he might have toward his brothers; he views things from a different perspective. He says later, "You meant evil against me, but God meant it for good" (50:20). It is not easy for anyone to lay aside a desire for revenge—especially when there has been real hurt. But the moment when a self-centered response seems reasonable is the very moment when a God-centered response is most needed.

Q: *Is there something going on in your life, your family, or your church that you need to apply this truth to?*

PRAY: *Father, help me to see your greater purposes in my daily struggles with others.*

Day 4

Taking revenge is the dark side of our inbuilt sense of justice. We long to see right done, so we think we should get on and do it ourselves.

ROMANS 12:18-21

Q: *What are Christians called to do (v 13)? Why might this seem impossible?*

Q: *How does the truth of v 19 help us control our instinct for revenge?*

We can't control what others think and do; we can only, with God's help, control ourselves. So we have to reconcile ourselves to the fact that we might have to live with fractured relationships and the hostility of others, perhaps for life. Even when our cause is justified, we must not take revenge. We can never understand everything about why a situation has developed. We don't know all the motives. So any revenge we might take on someone else—from legal prosecution to being cold and silent with them—will be flawed and imperfect. But we can trust God's judgment. He sees everything perfectly, and will exact precisely the right punishment for any crime—ours as well as others'. Knowing this truth will help us lay aside our feelings, and do something miraculous instead. To take revenge is to seek to take God's place. We have no right and no need to do that.

Q: *What should we do instead (v 20)? What is the principle we now work to (v 21)?*

PRAY: *Father, thank you that you are the perfect Judge. Help me to leave you to deal with the mess, and give me the strength to love others, as Jesus loved me.*

Day 5

Saul (Paul), the zealous persecutor of the first Christians, has been wonderfully converted. After fleeing from Damascus, he returns to Jerusalem for the first time as a believer.

ACTS 9:26-28

Q: *What was the reaction of the Christians in Jerusalem to Paul?*

Q: *Why might it have been difficult for Barnabas to take this initiative (see 8:3)?*

Q: *What was the result?*

You can't blame the Jerusalem disciples. They must have been terrified of Paul's reputation; he had been at the head of a ruthless and violent persecution that had scattered the Jerusalem fellowship far and wide. Saul had ravaged the church, going from house to house, dragging off men and women to prison. They may have thought his confession of faith was a ruse to expose more Christians. But Barnabas courageously crosses the divide. He could have been walking into a trap. He may have alienated himself from the other believers by his action. But his initiative reconciles the two groups. The result is that Saul's powerful gospel preaching and testimony are heard throughout the city.

Barnabas is a shining example of how to be a peacemaker. He risked himself in obedience to Jesus' command to love our enemies, and was an enormous blessing to everyone as a result.

PRAY: *Father, help me to be courageous as a peacemaker. Help me to cross boundaries of suspicion and fear to bring people together for the sake of your kingdom.*

Day 6

Sometimes reconciliation works. Sometimes it does not. It's the reality of the world we live in.

ACTS 15:37-40

Q: *What was the cause of the dispute? Why do you think it became so heated?*

Q: *What was the result? Was that a bad thing, do you think?*

This scene is all the more perplexing when you consider how Barnabas gave Paul the benefit of the doubt in Jerusalem. I suspect that passions grew because of the importance of the work: Paul did not want his mission to the Gentiles to be compromised by John Mark, who had "history." Barnabas was committed to giving him a second chance. So they split. Like many disputes between people—both Christian and not Christian—you can see both sides of this. Sometimes an entire church will split over what appear to be two godly but competing motives, leaving a huge amount of heartache and pain in its wake.

Any kind of division between Christians is painful, and yet, in God's mercy, here it was not a disaster. The split was not over doctrine but about a judgement call, and neither let it distract them from their efforts to spread the gospel. Years later, the rift seems to have healed (see 2 Timothy 4:11; Colossians 4:10). There will always be times when believers disagree on matters of opinion; what is important is that we remain focused on our mission, and open to reconciliation.

PRAY: *That the gospel would continue to flourish despite divisions among Christians.*

 **JOURNAL**

What I've learned or been particularly struck by this week…

What I want to change in my perspectives or actions as a result of this week…

Things I would like to think about more or discuss with others at my church…

BIBLE STUDY

Discuss

Think of a time when you were in need of reconciliation with someone else. What happened? How was the situation resolved? What was it that kept you apart for so long?

👉 READ PHILIPPIANS 4:2-7

2 I entreat Euodia and I entreat Syntyche to agree in the Lord. 3 Yes, I ask you also, true companion, help these women, who have labored side by side with me in the gospel together with Clement and the rest of my fellow workers, whose names are in the book of life.

1. What encouraging things do verses 2-3 tell us about the two women Euodia and Syntyche?

We don't know the details of their disagreement. Why do you think Paul steers clear of the nature of their disagreement?

2. What does it mean to "agree in the Lord" (v 2-3)?

Why is Paul so anxious for them to agree with each other (see also 2:3-5; 1:27)?

3. How can others be involved in helping their brothers and sisters to be reconciled (4:2-3)?

4. What clues are there in verses 4-7 about how we can be maintainers of peace, as well as makers of it?

5. Paul's advice is for Christians helping other Christians to reconcile. How might we help reconcile family, friends, work colleagues or people in our community who may not be believers?

6. Think again about some of the situations you discussed or thought about in the opening question. What pieces of Paul's godly wisdom might have made the situation better?

Apply

FOR YOURSELF: Choose one character trait of a "peacemaker" from question 4. How can you help yourself to grow in this?

FOR YOUR CHURCH: Are there any divisions between people or groups in your church, perhaps that have gone on for a long time? It is a problem for all of you. How will you pursue reconciliation as those whose names are "in the book of life" (v 3)?

IN YOUR NATION: How can you be a voice for reconciliation in your community or on a wider stage in your country? What is one positive step you can take to be part of the solution, and not the problem?

Pray

FOR YOUR CHURCH: Pray for any situations you have discussed where there is still no reconciliation. Pray especially that peacemakers and church leaders might take the initiative to restore people to love and fellowship with each other.

FOR THOSE YOU KNOW: Pray for marriages, parents and children, and whole families known to you where there is the pain of broken relationships. Pray for forgiveness, healing, and hope.

FOR YOUR COMMUNITY: Pray for community leaders, politicians and national leaders—that they would seek peace and the common good, especially in places and countries where there are deep divisions and painful histories.

SERMON NOTES

Bible passage:

Date:

SESSION 7:

DIVERSITY: COMMUNITY ENRICHED

FOR THE MOST PART, THE WESTERN WORLD IS NOW ALLERGIC TO STATEMENTS, POLICIES, IDEOLOGIES AND GROUPS THAT ARE ACTIVELY OPPOSED TO DIVERSITY. BUT THERE'S A HUGE DIFFERENCE BETWEEN TALKING ABOUT DIVERSITY AND ACTUALLY EMBRACING IT. AND THAT'S A PROBLEM IN OUR CHURCHES TOO. TO HELP US, WE'LL TAKE ANOTHER THRILLING LOOK AT WHERE OUR GOSPEL COMMUNITIES ARE HEADING – TO GOD'S PERFECT SHALOM-SHAPED NEW CREATION.

DIVERSITY: COMMUNITY ENRICHED

Discuss

This session is titled "Diversity: Community Enriched." Is your local community currently enriched by diversity? If so, how?

_____

_____

_____

_____

▶ WATCH DVD 7.1 OR LISTEN TO TALK 7.1

_____

_____

_____

_____

_____

_____

☛ LUKE 10:29-37

29 But he, desiring to justify himself, said to Jesus, "And who is my neighbor?" 30 Jesus replied, "A man was going down from Jerusalem to Jericho, and he fell among robbers, who stripped him and beat him and departed, leaving him half dead. 31 Now by chance a priest was going down that road, and when he saw him he passed by on the other side. 32 So likewise a Levite, when he came to the place and saw him, passed by on the other side. 33 But a Samaritan, as he journeyed, came to where he was, and when he saw him, he had compassion. [34] He went to him and bound up his wounds, pouring on oil and wine. Then he set him on his own animal and brought him to an inn and took care of him. [35] And the next day he took out two denarii and gave them to the innkeeper, saying, 'Take care of him, and whatever more you spend, I will repay you when I come back.' [36] Which of these three, do you think, proved to be a neighbor to the man who fell among the robbers?" [37] He said, "The one who showed him mercy." And Jesus said to him, "You go, and do likewise."

Discuss

What question did the lawyer ask Jesus (verse 29)? How did he then answer his own question (verses 36-37)?

_____

_____

_____

Jesus' parable doesn't tell us "who" our neighbor is so much as "how" to be a neighbor. How are we to be neighbors to others? How do we know from the parable that this applies to more than just those who live close to us?

_____

_____

_____

☛ REVELATION 7:9-14

[9] After this I looked, and behold, a great multitude that no one could number, from every nation, from all tribes and peoples and languages, standing before the throne and before the Lamb, clothed in white robes, with palm branches in their hands, [10] and crying out with a loud voice, "Salvation belongs to our God who sits on the throne, and to the Lamb!" [11] And all the angels were standing around the throne and around the elders and the four living creatures, and they fell on their faces before the throne and worshiped God, [12] saying, "Amen! Blessing and glory and wisdom and thanksgiving and honor and power and might be to our God forever and ever! Amen."

13 Then one of the elders addressed me, saying, "Who are these, clothed in white robes, and from where have they come?" 14 I said to him, "Sir, you know." And he said to me, "These are the ones coming out of the great tribulation. They have washed their robes and made them white in the blood of the Lamb.

▶ **WATCH DVD 7.2 OR LISTEN TO TALK 7.2**

_____

_____

_____

_____

_____

_____

_____

_____

_____

Discuss

In Revelation 7, John sees a huge crowd standing before God's throne. Where are they from (verse 9)? How does one of the elders describe these people (verse 14)?

_____

_____

_____

What does John's vision have to do with the issue of diversity?

_____

_____

_____

Use the following questions from Stephen Um's talk to ask yourselves how well your church family is modeling this "unity-in-diversity":

- Who do you go to church with? Is it primarily people that look like you, and talk like you?
- What is the ethnic makeup of your congregation in comparison to the ethnic makeup of your neighborhood?
- Are you cultivating friendships with people in your congregation who are unlike you—a different generation; a different socio-economic group; a different ethnicity?
- Who do you spend your time with during the week? Who are your closest friends? Are they those who look and act like you? Do you have close friends who are radically different than you?

▶ **WATCH DVD 7.3 OR LISTEN TO TALK 7.3**

_____

_____

_____

_____

Discuss

"The book of Revelation gives us a picture of what happens when God makes the world right. It is ultimately a foretelling of God's inevitable victory. In the end, GOD WINS and brings about the holistic shalom that he desires. He wants unity-in-diversity in his people—and he is going to get it."

How do you respond to this statement, and why?

_____

_____

_____

_____

_____

Look again at your answers to the "unity-in-diversity" questions on page 138. What practical steps can you take to open up relationships with those who are unlike you? Include at least one idea that you can put into practice in the next 24 hours.

_____

_____

_____

_____

_____

_____

Look back over your notes and journal from the previous sessions.

• What are some of the things you have been challenged to do as an individual so that you reflect God's mercy to those around you?

• What are some of the changes you could make as a church family to model mercy and work toward *shalom* in your neighborhood?

Pray

👉 **REVELATION 7:9-10**

⁹ *After this I looked, and behold, a great multitude that no one could number, from every nation, from all tribes and peoples and languages, standing before the throne and before the Lamb, clothed in white robes, with palm branches in their hands,* ¹⁰ *and crying out with a loud voice, "Salvation belongs to our God who sits on the throne, and to the Lamb!"*

Thank the Lord that, because of Jesus, you can look forward to being part of the great multitude standing before the throne and praising him.

Look at some of the practical things you have written on this page. Pray that you will be able to put these into practice to reflect God's mercy and bring *shalom* to this world.

DAILY BIBLE DEVOTIONALS

Our destiny is to be a richly diverse people in the new creation, united in Christ. These readings trace the story of unity and diversity through the Bible.

Day 1

GENESIS 11:1-9

Q: *What were the people attempting to do when they built the city and its tower?*

Q: *Why was this so bad (see Genesis 1:28)?*

Q: *What was the result of God's confusion of their language?*

The clue is in the phrases "make a name for ourselves" and that the tower was built into the heavens. This is the desire to be like God that was Adam and Eve's undoing in Eden, but multiplied exponentially. They were unified in a desire to be like God and to take the glory of God to themselves. God sees the danger of this—not to him, but to the people he made and loves. Their ambition was truly evil, and so would be truly self-destructive. So, for their sake, he frustrates their ambition with the "curse" of languages. They are scattered and spread throughout the world. So the diversity of cultures and language we see throughout the world is God's doing, for our good and for protection from ourselves. We find out why tomorrow.

Q: *How does this thought change the way we might view other cultures?*

PRAY: *Praise God that the diversity in the world is his doing, and for our benefit.*

Day 2

ACTS 17:22-31

Many millennia have passed since the dawn of diversity at the tower of Babel. Paul stands in a marketplace in Athens and delivers a powerful message to the people around him.

Q: *What is the thrust of his message?*

Q: *What insights does he have about how God has ordered the world (v 26, 27)?*

It is the year of the Lord's favor (v 30). Although people have ignorantly worshiped idols and false gods, the time of guessing about God is over now that Jesus has come. Intriguingly, Paul suggests that all history has been building to this point. Different nations and people have come and gone, but it is all a part of the deliberate plan of God. We are made who we are and placed where we are so that we might seek God. In some way the diversity of the human race is part of the way that God is leading us toward him. And now that Jesus has been revealed and the coming judgment has been authenticated by his resurrection, it is time to respond to God's loving grace.

Q: *Does this thought change the way you think about your national history, and the history of other cultures?*

PRAY: *Thank God that he is powerfully at work in the founding and making of nations.*

Day 3

GALATIANS 3:7-9

Q: *Who are the true children of Abraham, according to Paul in these verses?*

Q: *Why is that so important for the Gentile and Jewish believers he is writing to?*

Paul is arguing against the false sense of superiority that Jewish Christians felt over Gentile Christians. Jewish people had long considered themselves special as "children of the promise" given to Abraham in Genesis 12:1-3. But Paul's argument here is that God is preaching the gospel to Abraham in these verses when he says that "in you shall all the nations be blessed." Yes, Israel had a privileged position, but now the gospel is for all mankind—every family on earth. The inclusion of all nations was part of his plan from the very beginning, not an afterthought.

Now that humankind is being re-created as we are joined to Jesus—the perfect man—so the forces that drove us apart at Babel are being reversed. On the day of Pentecost (Acts 2), when the Spirit fell on the first believers, they spoke in tongues so that *everyone* could understand them. The gospel of Jesus was proclaimed to the nations and the confusion of Babel was undone. A diverse but unified church is a compelling and powerful sign of God's plan and our future.

Q: *Are there unhelpful ways of thinking about race or class that you have absorbed from your culture or family, which are in opposition to the gospel plan of God?*

PRAY: *Thank you that I am united with my brothers and sisters throughout the world. Help me to rejoice in your plan for the world.*

Day 4

GALATIANS 3:27-29

Q: *What is Paul saying in verse 28?*

Q: *Where does this countercultural unity come from?*

As believers in Christ, we have more in common with each other than through any of our other identities: race, nationality, social status or gender. Christians have been gifted the kind of liberty, equality and fraternity that the world hungers for, and attempts to create by other means. Human efforts to do this can result in a drive for uniformity, where differences are suppressed, or else diversity becomes its own god. We are urged to worship diversity instead of the One who created it.

But Paul is saying that the gospel leads to a unique diverse unity. We don't diminish differences; we rejoice in them as gifts of God. One of the main points of Paul's letter to the Galatians is that Greek Christians do not need to become Jewish Christians. But he doesn't mean that there should be no distinctions between our roles as male and female, or employer and employee in the way we live.

Our unity comes from the amazing privilege of our sonship in Christ, which is greater than any earthly advantage or disadvantage. That is why there is no place for pride in our race or status. We are joined to Jesus and each other by grace alone, through faith alone.

PRAY: *Lord, help me to rejoice in those you have called to eternal life with me.*

Day 5

It is a common accusation that the church is so divided that it is not worth bothering with. As believers we also feel these things deeply. What hope is there for our unity?

JOHN 17:20-21

Q: *Who is Jesus praying for?*

Q: *What specific things does he ask God to do in and through his people?*

Of course, visibly, Christian churches are divided along lines of style and culture, as well as on more substantial theological issues. But what Jesus says is that this disunity is illusory. True Christians, who are in Jesus, are united in the same way that Jesus and his Father are united. You and I are joined together as intimately as the persons of the Trinity are united.

We may struggle with the difficulties of disunity, but we can never be without hope—because Jesus is praying for us! If it were down to our own efforts, we would inevitably fly apart in self-centered dislike of people different than ourselves. Growing in mutual love and unity is growing to be what we truly are—not an endless fight to maintain something that is unnatural.

Q: *What is at stake with our Christian unity?*

Our visible unity in diversity is an inherent part of our witness to the reality of who Jesus is. Our one-ness will lead people to believe that Jesus is the Christ.

PRAY: *Lord Jesus, make my church a living demonstration of who you are, so that people would believe in you by our unity.*

Day 6

REVELATION 7:9-10

Q: *What is encouraging about this vision of the eternity that God has planned for us?*

Q: *In what ways should this vision inform how we live now, do you think?*

- **There is a multitude:** We often think we are few in number; but God is amazingly gracious and filled with mercy. That will be evident in the new creation.
- **From every nation, people, tribe, and language:** There will be no unreached peoples in eternity. The new creation will be a treasure house of all that is wonderful in this world, but better—because there will be none of the bad stuff along with it.
- **Standing before the throne:** We have been brought close through Christ, but God can feel distant as we trust his promise by faith; but then we will see him face to face.
- **Clothed in white robes:** We are forgiven, but still struggle with our old life. Then we will be free of all the sin.
- **Shouting with a loud voice:** Now we are often heavy-hearted, and struggle to praise God and give him the glory. Then we will praise God with glorious abandon.

This is the life we are preparing for, so let's share the gospel, be united with our true family, draw close to God, fight against sin, and praise God in anticipation of all that is to come.

PRAY: *Sing along with the heavenly choir: "Salvation belongs to our God who sits on the throne, and to the Lamb!"*

JOURNAL

What I've learned or been particularly struck by this week...

_____

_____

_____

_____

_____

_____

What I want to change in my perspectives or actions as a result of this week...

_____

_____

_____

_____

_____

_____

Things I would like to think about more or discuss with others at my church...

_____

_____

_____

_____

_____

_____

BIBLE STUDY

Discuss

The Bible presents us with a breathtaking vision of God's ultimate plan for the world: a new community of God's people from every nation, tribe and level of society, united in Christ forever. But Christians have often struggled to live out the reality of God's global plan in our churches today.

Why do we prefer to spend time with "people like us"? Is that a good or a bad thing?

How can this happen in churches? Is that a good or bad thing?

 READ ACTS 11:1-18

¹ Now the apostles and the brothers who were throughout Judea heard that the Gentiles also had received the word of God. ² So when Peter went up to Jerusalem, the circumcision party criticized him, saying, ³ "You went to uncircumcised men and ate with them."

This is a report of what happened to Peter when God led him to share the gospel with Cornelius—a God-fearing Gentile, as reported in greater detail in the rest of chapter 11. This is a very big moment in the life of the early church.

1. Why was this event such a big deal for the early church?

_____

_____

What hints and indications does the Old Testament give that the gospel is for the whole world? What should Peter, as a Jew, have already known? (See Isaiah 42:5-7; Psalm 67; Acts 1:8; 8:4-8, 27; John 10:16; 12:20-23; Matthew 15:22-28; Jonah.)

_____

_____

_____

2. What does the reaction of the "circumcision party" show about their understanding (Acts 11:2-3)?

How do they respond when they hear the full story (v 17-18)?

READ ACTS 11:19-26

19 Now those who were scattered because of the persecution that arose over Stephen traveled as far as Phoenicia and Cyprus and Antioch, speaking the word to no one except Jews. 20 But there were some of them, men of Cyprus and Cyrene, who on coming to Antioch spoke to the Hellenists also...

3. What happened in Antioch that confirmed what started with Cornelius?

4. What signs can you think of from the rest of the New Testament that, as the church continued to grow and spread, it was marked by both its enormous diversity and its wonderful unity in Christ?

How can this rich diversity be such a powerful testimony to the grace of God both then and today?

5. What signs can you think of in the rest of the New Testament that it remained a struggle to strive for this unity in diversity?

Apply

FOR YOUR CHURCH: Where do we feel the same pressures today in our churches? How can you protect yourself from slipping back into worldly ways of thinking in this area?

IN YOUR COMMUNITY: This miraculous unity in diversity in Christ is something which is a unique gift to the church. But Christians should also be working to establish the equality and validity of every person in society. How does 2 Corinthians 5:14-16 help us see why we should be involved in this wider work?

FOR YOURSELF: What simple practical things can you do that will encourage the practice of a godly diversity in your church and in society?

Pray

FOR YOURSELF: Pray that you would learn to silence your instinctive reactions to people who are different, and praise God for his love for all people. Pray that you would view all people as precious souls made in the image of God and in need of Christ's forgiveness.

FOR YOUR CHURCH: Pray that your church would become a richly diverse community that delights in God's grace and calling.

SERMON NOTES

Bible passage: Date:

GOSPEL SHAPED

CHURCH

The Complete Series

LET THE POWER OF THE GOSPEL SHAPE
FOUR OTHER CRITICAL AREAS IN
THE LIFE OF YOUR CHURCH

"WE WANT CHURCHES CALLED INTO EXISTENCE BY THE GOSPEL TO BE SHAPED BY THE GOSPEL IN THEIR EVERYDAY LIFE."

DON CARSON AND TIM KELLER

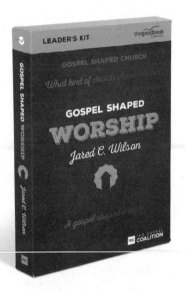

GOSPEL SHAPED
WORSHIP

Christians are people who have discovered that the one true object of our worship is the God who has revealed himself in and through Jesus Christ.

But what exactly is worship? What should we be doing when we meet together for "church" on Sundays? And how does that connect with what we do the rest of the week?

This seven-week whole-church curriculum explores what it means to be a worshiping community. As we search the Scriptures together, we will discover that true worship must encompass the whole of life. This engaging and flexible resource will challenge us to worship God every day of the week, with all our heart, mind, soul and strength.

Written and presented by **JARED C. WILSON**
Jared is Director of Communications at Midwestern Seminary and College in Kansas City, and a prolific author. He is married to Becky and they have two daughters.

WWW.GOSPELSHAPEDCHURCH.ORG/WORSHIP

GOSPEL SHAPED
OUTREACH

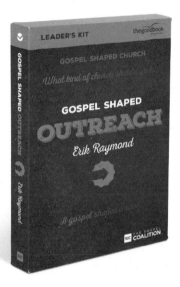

Many Christians are nervous about telling someone else about Jesus. The nine sessions in this curriculum don't offer quick fixes or evangelism "gimmicks." But by continually pointing us back to the gospel, they will give us the proper motivation to work together as a church to share the gospel message with those who are lost without Christ.

As you work through the material, you will discover that God's mission of salvation in the world is also your mission; and that he is inviting you into the privilege of praying and working to advance his kingdom among your family, friends, neighbors, co-workers and community.

Gospel Shaped Church is a curriculum from The Gospel Coalition that will help whole congregations pause and think slowly, carefully and prayerfully about the kind of church they are called to be.

Written and presented by **ERIK RAYMOND**
Erik is the Preaching Pastor at Emmaus Bible Church in Omaha, Nebraska. He is married to Christie and they have six children.

WWW.GOSPELSHAPEDCHURCH.ORG/OUTREACH

GOSPEL SHAPED
LIVING

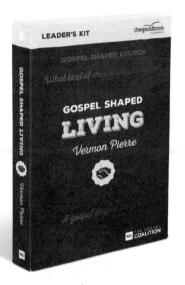

Start a fresh discussion in your church about how the gospel of Christ impacts every area of life in our world.

Gospel Shaped Living explores over seven sessions what it means for a local church to be a distinctive, counter-cultural community.

Through the gospel, God calls people from every nation, race and background to be joined together in a new family that shows his grace and glory. How should our lives as individuals and as a church reflect and model the new life we have found in Christ? And how different should we be to the world around us?

This challenging and interactive course will inspire us to celebrate grace and let the gospel shape our lives day by day.

Written and presented by **VERMON PIERRE**
Vermon is the Lead Pastor of Roosevelt Community Church in Phoenix, Arizona, and a Gospel Coalition council member. He is married to Dennae and they have four children.

WWW.GOSPELSHAPEDCHURCH.ORG/LIVING

"THESE RESOURCES GIVE SPACE TO CONSIDER WHAT A GENUINE EXPRESSION OF A GOSPEL-SHAPED CHURCH LOOKS LIKE FOR YOU IN THE PLACE GOD HAS PUT YOU, AND WITH THE PEOPLE HE HAS GATHERED INTO FELLOWSHIP WITH YOU."

DON CARSON AND TIM KELLER

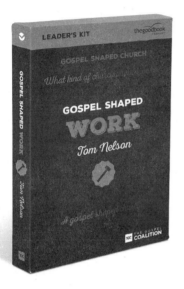

GOSPEL SHAPED
WORK

Many Christians experience a troubling disconnect between their everyday work and what they live and work for as a believer in Jesus. How should the gospel shape my view of life on an assembly line, or change my work as a teacher, artist, nurse, home-maker or gardener?

Gospel Shaped Work explores over eight sessions how the gospel changes the way we view our work in the world—and how a church should equip its members to serve God in their everyday vocations, and relate to the wider world of work.

These engaging and practical sessions reveal the Bible's all-encompassing vision for our daily lives, and our engagement with culture as a redeemed community. They will provoke a fresh discussion in your church about how the gospel of Christ impacts every area of life in our world.

Written and presented by **TOM NELSON**
Tom is the Senior Pastor of Christ Community Church in Kansas City, and president of *Made To Flourish network*. He is married to Liz and they have two grown children.

WWW.GOSPELSHAPEDCHURCH.ORG/WORK

THE GOSPEL
COALITION

This set of resources is based on the five principles of gospel-centered ministry as laid out in The Gospel Coalition's foundation documents. The text reads:

What is gospel–centered ministry?
It is characterized by:

1. Empowered corporate worship
The gospel changes our relationship with God from one of hostility or slavish compliance to one of intimacy and joy. The core dynamic of gospel–centered ministry is therefore worship and fervent prayer. In corporate worship God's people receive a special life–transforming sight of the worth and beauty of God, and then give back to God suitable expressions of his worth. At the heart of corporate worship is the ministry of the Word. Preaching should be expository (explaining the text of Scripture) and Christ–centered (expounding all biblical themes as climaxing in Christ and his work of salvation). Its ultimate goal, however, is not simply to teach but to lead the hearers to worship, individual and corporate, that strengthens their inner being to do the will of God.

2. Evangelistic effectiveness
Because the gospel (unlike religious moralism) produces people who do not disdain those who disagree with them, a truly gospel–centered church should be filled with members who winsomely address people's hopes and aspirations with Christ and his saving work. We have a vision for a church that sees conversions of rich and poor, highly educated and less educated, men and women, old and young, married and single, and all races. We hope to draw highly secular and postmodern people, as well as reaching religious and traditional people. Because of the attractiveness of its community and the humility of its people, a gospel–centered

church should find people in its midst who are exploring and trying to understand Christianity. It must welcome them in hundreds of ways. It will do little to make them "comfortable" but will do much to make its message understandable. In addition to all this, gospel–centered churches will have a bias toward church planting as one of the most effective means of evangelism there is.

3. Counter–cultural community
Because the gospel removes both fear and pride, people should get along inside the church who could never get along outside. Because it points us to a man who died for his enemies, the gospel creates relationships of service rather than of selfishness. Because the gospel calls us to holiness, the people of God live in loving bonds of mutual accountability and discipline. Thus the gospel creates a human community radically different from any society around it. Regarding sex, the church should avoid both the secular society's idolization of sex and traditional society's fear of it. It is a community which so loves and cares practically for its members that biblical chastity makes sense. It teaches its members to conform their bodily being to the shape of the gospel—abstinence outside of heterosexual marriage and fidelity and joy within. Regarding the family, the church should affirm the goodness of marriage between a man and a woman, calling them to serve God by reflecting his covenant love in life–long loyalty, and by teaching his ways to their children. But it also affirms the goodness of serving Christ as singles, whether for a time or for a life. The church should surround all persons suffering from the fallenness of our human sexuality with a compassionate

community and family. Regarding money, the church's members should engage in radical economic sharing with one another—so "there are no needy among them" (Acts 4:34). Such sharing also promotes a radically generous commitment of time, money, relationships, and living space to social justice and the needs of the poor, the oppressed, the immigrant, and the economically and physically weak. Regarding power, it is visibly committed to power-sharing and relationship-building among races, classes, and generations that are alienated outside of the Body of Christ. The practical evidence of this is that our local churches increasingly welcome and embrace people of all races and cultures. Each church should seek to reflect the diversity of its local geographical community, both in the congregation at large and in its leadership.

4. The integration of faith and work

The good news of the Bible is not only individual forgiveness but the renewal of the whole creation. God put humanity in the garden to cultivate the material world for his own glory and for the flourishing of nature and the human community. The Spirit of God not only converts individuals (e.g., John 16:8) but also renews and cultivates the face of the earth (e.g., Gen 1:2; Psalm 104:30). Therefore Christians glorify God not only through the ministry of the Word, but also through their vocations of agriculture, art, business, government, scholarship—all for God's glory and the furtherance of the public good. Too many Christians have learned to seal off their faith-beliefs from the way they work in their vocation. The gospel is seen as a means of finding individual peace and not as the foundation of a worldview—a comprehensive interpretation of reality affecting all that we do. But we have a vision for a church that equips its people to think out the implications of the gospel on how we do carpentry, plumbing, data-entry, nursing, art, business, government, journalism, entertainment, and scholarship. Such a church will not only support Christians' engagement with culture, but will also help them work with distinctiveness, excellence, and accountability in their trades and professions. Developing humane yet creative and excellent business environments out of our understanding of the gospel is part of the work of bringing a measure of healing to God's creation in the power of the Spirit. Bringing Christian joy, hope, and truth to embodiment in the arts is also part of this work. We do all of this because the gospel of God leads us to it, even while we recognize that the ultimate restoration of all things awaits the personal and bodily return of our Lord Jesus Christ

5. The doing of justice and mercy

God created both soul and body, and the resurrection of Jesus shows that he is going to redeem both the spiritual and the material. Therefore God is concerned not only for the salvation of souls but also for the relief of poverty, hunger, and injustice. The gospel opens our eyes to the fact that all our wealth (even wealth for which we worked hard) is ultimately an unmerited gift from God. Therefore the person who does not generously give away his or her wealth to others is not merely lacking in compassion, but is unjust. Christ wins our salvation through losing, achieves power through weakness and service, and comes to wealth through giving all away. Those who receive his salvation are not the strong and accomplished but those who admit they are weak and lost. We cannot look at the poor and the oppressed and callously call them to pull themselves out of their own difficulty. Jesus did not treat us that way. The gospel replaces superiority toward the poor with mercy and compassion. Christian churches must work for justice and peace in their neighborhoods through service even as they call individuals to conversion and the new birth. We must work for the eternal and common good and show our neighbors we love them sacrificially whether they believe as we do or not. Indifference to the poor and disadvantaged means there has not been a true grasp of our salvation by sheer grace.

thegoodbook
COMPANY

Opening up the Bible

At The Good Book Company, we are dedicated to helping Christians and local churches grow. We believe that God's growth process always starts with hearing clearly what he has said to us through his timeless word—the Bible.

Ever since we opened our doors in 1991, we have been striving to produce resources that honour God in the way the Bible is used. We have grown to become an international provider of user-friendly resources to the Christian community, with believers of all backgrounds and denominations using our Bible studies, books, evangelistic resources, DVD-based courses and training events.

We want to equip ordinary Christians to live for Christ day by day, and churches to grow in their knowledge of God, their love for one another, and the effectiveness of their outreach.

Call us for a discussion of your needs or visit one of our local websites for more information on the resources and services we provide.

Your friends at The Good Book Company

NORTH AMERICA		thegoodbook.com		866 244 2165
UK & EUROPE		thegoodbook.co.uk		0333 123 0880
AUSTRALIA		thegoodbook.com.au		(02) 6100 4211
NEW ZEALAND		thegoodbook.co.nz		(+64) 3 343 2463

WWW.CHRISTIANITYEXPLORED.ORG
Our partner site is a great place for those exploring the Christian faith, with a clear explanation of the good news, powerful testimonies and answers to difficult questions.